FiEsTa
ON THE GRILL

FiEsTa ON THE GRILL

Daniel Hoyer

Photographs by Marty Snortum

Gibbs Smith, Publisher
Salt Lake City

This book is dedicated to my two Dachshunds, Layla and Koko, who were repeatedly tormented by the aromas of grilled and smoked meats cooking on the patio. Their uncritical appreciation of my recipes is always an inspiration.

First Edition
10 09 08 07 06   5 4 3 2 1

Text © 2006 Daniel Hoyer
Photographs © 2006 Marty Snortum

Published by
Gibbs Smith, Publisher
P.O. Box 667
Layton, Utah 84041

Orders: 1.800.748.5439
www.gibbs-smith.com

Designed by Dawn DeVries Sokol
Printed and bound in Hong Kong

Library of Congress Cataloging-in-Publication Data

Hoyer, Daniel.
  Fiesta on the grill / Daniel Hoyer ; photographs by Marty Snortum.— 1st ed.
     p. cm.
  ISBN 1-58685-376-7
  1. Barbecue cookery. 2. Cookery, American—Southwestern style. 3. Cookery, Latin American. I. Title.

TX840.B3H69 2006
641.5'784—dc22

                                                2006007039

cONTeNtS

INtRODucTiON

History

Cooking, grilling and smoking over an open fire or coals presumably were all developed shortly after humans first discovered how to tame fire itself. The process was probably part design, part accident. I imagine that the revelation that by exposing the meat from hunted wild game to the heat and smoke of the fire and finding you could not only preserve the meat but also dramatically improve its flavor was nothing short of momentous. A better understanding of the science involved and some technical improvements have been achieved since then, such as vessels for containing the fire, grates and spits for more conveniently and safely holding meats over the fire while being cooked, containers to trap the smoke for slow cooking and convenience fuels like charcoal, gas and briquettes. Despite the vast amount of history since that original discovery, outdoor cooking has remained remarkably, in essence, the same for many millennia.

Most cultures throughout the world carry on a tradition of grilling over an open fire with varying degrees of sophistication. In North America, a renaissance has taken place in backyard grilling and barbecue that has become an indispensable part of our cooking culture. Many restaurants now feature menu items from the char grill and the use of natural fuels has regained a chic status in these commercial venues.

In Latin America, the practice of grilling also remains popular. Market and street-side food vendors often prepare meat, poultry, seafood and vegetables *a la parrilla*, or over the grating or grill, for their hungry clientele. Special celebrations, or fiestas, frequently include foods cooked on an outdoor fire or in a fire pit that was created impromptu, just for the occasion. In the less developed regions, a natural fire may be the only method available or affordable for food preparation. The Spanish word *barbacoa* is thought to derive from the Arawak or Carib indigenous people's languages and is believed to be the root of the English word *barbecue*.

With such a long and illustrious history, we have many options in our approach to outdoor cooking. I have chosen to draw on flavors of the New World, Latin America, the Caribbean and the American Southwest as my inspiration for these grilling recipes. You will find traditional preparations, popular contemporary versions and some of my own original grilling concoctions, using the bold and exciting flavors of these regions. Along with the recipes cooked on the grill, I have included some dishes that are well suited to complement and complete a grilled menu. Let's fire up those grills and get cooking!

Techniques

Fuels and Types of Grills

There is nothing quite like the taste that is achieved by cooking over flames and coals. The direct heat browns the meat and adds caramelized flavors and the smoke contributes a seductive acridity and richness. The use of natural fuels certainly develops the very best flavors; however, the convenience of gas grills and their accurate heat controls make them very appealing, and the result is still very good. Some will argue that the odor additives in natural and LP gas taint the flavor of gas-grilled foods; but I think that it takes an extremely sensitive or discerning palate to actually detect any negative flavors. The rustic smoky flavors imparted by wood or charcoal are only less pronounced with gas.

Grill styles range from a small barrel or hole in the ground with a grate over the top to charcoal-fired, small hibachis, kettles, rectangle or half-barrel backyard varieties all the way to sophisticated, high-tech, multi-control gas cookers and infinite variations in between. A fairly recent innovation in wood-fired grills is offered by Traeger Industries. Their natural, wood pellet grills feature electric starters, a hopper that stores and automatically feeds the fuel and a thermostat to control the whole process. This type of grill may be used for both direct cooking and smoking, some of the best of both worlds. Whatever grill style you choose, it is important to have a system for regulating the heat and the ability to create different

Fuel choices for grilling (from upper left, clockwise): chunk charcoal, wood chips, charcoal briquettes, wood chunks and compressed natural wood pellets

heat zones for a varied cooking approach. A lid is a nice option but is only essential if you are smoking or slow roasting with your grill or cooking outdoors in foul weather. Although not the ideal grill, an indoor, ridged, stovetop grill can be useful when you just cannot cook outdoors. It does impart some grilled-type flavor and allows for the low-fat style of cooking akin to an outdoor grill.

Wood for Cooking or As a Flavoring

Natural hardwoods can be used as the main fuel source or as a flavor enhancer when cooking with charcoal or gas. Soft or overly resinous wood such as pine, cedar, aspen, etc., should be avoided as they contain a lot of creosote and burn quickly while imparting a kerosene-like taste to food. Oak and hickory are full-flavored, yet on the mild side; fruitwoods and wood from nut trees like pecan are a bit stronger and often add a touch of sweetness; alder is stronger yet; and mesquite is one of the more powerful flavors of wood suitable for cooking. There are also many local varieties of wood you may choose, just make sure the flavor of the wood matches or complements the food to be cooked. There is no need to soak wood that is the primary fuel for grilling, although some cooks do like to soak their wood chunks or chips when using them to enhance the flavor while grilling or smoking with charcoal or gas. The soaking slows down the speed at which the wood burns and produces more smoke. I usually only soak my wood chunks to conserve fuel when I am preparing a recipe that requires an extended cooking time. When using natural wood pellets, like the fuel required for the Traeger self-feeding grill, nothing needs to be done to the fuel other than to select the proper wood variety for the desired flavor.

Charcoal and Briquettes

Natural lump charcoal is becoming widely available and is an excellent fuel for grilling. It burns hot, clean, and imparts a subtle smoky flavor to food. Charcoal briquettes are the most common fuel used in the United States and are available almost everywhere. They are easy to light and create a nice even heat. Some lower-priced briquettes have a lot of additives and binders so it is important to make sure that they are fully burned down to coals before you start cooking over them. When using either type of charcoal, you may want to add wood chunks or chips as an additional flavoring. To do this, start the charcoal and allow it to burn until there are no flames remaining and most of the charcoal has turned gray and is glowing. Add the wood just before you start cooking. For a hot fire, you will want to have two to three layers of charcoal; for a slower fire, one layer will usually suffice.

NOTE: You may also mix natural wood chunks along with either type of charcoal as a primary fuel. In this case, start the wood at the same time.

Starting the Fire

Always consult the manufacturer's instructions before lighting your grill. Most gas grills have a lighting system built in, although many I have used are easier to start with a match or lighter.

To start a wood or charcoal fire you can use lighter fluid, an electric starter or a chimney-type starter. When using lighter fluid, you should always let the flames burn down completely so that no flavor from the starting fluid is imparted to your food. After the flames subside, allow the coals to burn until a fine gray ash is formed over most of the charcoal and the desired temperature is reached.

NOTE: *Always leave the lid of the grill open when starting and during the initial burning of the coals.*

COOKING METHODS

Several different methods may be employed when cooking on a grill: direct grilling, indirect grilling, smoking, roasting and, with a little improvisation, baking.This book deals primarily with direct grilling, followed by smoking and a little of the rest.

Direct grilling, as the name implies, is cooking directly over the source of heat. This can be at high, medium or low temperatures. With this method, especially at the higher heat levels, the meat is seared and develops a rich caramelized flavor and color, and gets that distinct, charred flavor that we all love. This procedure also helps to keep the natural juices sealed in during the relatively short cooking time.

Indirect grilling is a slower process and is used for more delicate ingredients or meats that require a slower cooking time to develop tenderness. For this method, a fire is built in one section while the section to be cooked over has no fire. With a gas grill, this is accomplished by only lighting part of the burners. A lidded grill is helpful for indirect grilling. Roasting is similar to indirect grilling but uses even lower heat, a longer cooking time and a lid or cover

is required. To bake with your grill you will need to experiment with the cover and the fuels to reach and hold the correct temperature.

Cooking Temperatures

A thermometer is always handy for smoking, slow cooking and roasting; however, for direct grilling, the best technique is the counting method as the thermometer in the lid of a grill is not a good indicator of the heat at grill level. To test the heat with this system, hold your hand just above the cooking surface. For the high heat required to cook steaks, seafood, etc., you should only be able to hold your hand comfortably in that spot for about 3 to 4 seconds, for medium heat 5 to 7 seconds, and for low heat 8 to 12 seconds.

NOTE: *These are full seconds (one thousand one, one thousand two, etc.).*

TEMPERING MEATS BEFORE COOKING AND RESTING AFTER COOKING

Most meats, especially red meats, will cook better if they are tempered, or warmed a little before cooking. This allows the meat to cook more evenly and you will not have to overcook the outer portion before the center is done to your liking. It is important to keep your food safe during this process, as bacteria are more likely to multiply at warmer temperatures. This is especially critical with raw poultry. You do not need to warm it up to room temperature, only 10 to 15 degrees above what is was in the refrigerator. Anywhere from 15 to 30 minutes is usually enough.

Resting Meats after Cooking

No, the meat has not gotten tired. When meat is cooking, the individual cells expand due to the constant rise in temperature. After the meat is done, if you cut it immediately, the juices will flow out and you will lose both flavor and moisture. If you allow the meat to cool just slightly for a few minutes (I usually cover it loosely), the cells will contract and retain their juices. The time varies from 2 to 4 minutes for a steak, fish fillet or chicken breast up to 15 or 20 minutes for a whole brisket or turkey. This applies to meats that are served whole to be cut by each individual guest or meats that are carved prior to serving.

BRINING

Many smoking and some grilling recipes call for brining the meat. Brining was originally a method used to aid with preservation, but it also helps with flavor and creates a more tender and juicy product. Brining is accomplished by immersing the meat in a salt-water solution. Over time, the salt water is absorbed into the cells of the meat through osmosis. Sugar and other spices and herbs may also be added to the brine to enhance the flavors. Poultry seems to benefit the most from brining, followed by

Brining chicken for smoking

pork. Typically, brine has ½ to 1 cup of salt per gallon of water. You should refrigerate the brining meat during the process.

CHILE AND PEPPER ROASTING

Fresh chiles are often fire roasted to remove the skin, begin the cooking process and to give them a smoky and slightly sweeter flavor. They are usually charred and then peeled and seeded. This method also works for *chiles dulces,* or sweet bell peppers.

Place the chile over a direct flame or as near to a direct source of intense heat as possible (charcoal or gas grill, open gas burner, or oven broiler) and char the skin until at least 80 to 90 percent of the skin is blistered and blackened. Rotate often to cook evenly. Place in a paper or plastic bag or in a bowl covered with a kitchen towel or plastic wrap to trap the steam. This will loosen the skin and continue cooking the chile. After 10 to 15 minutes, rub the chile surface with a cloth or paper towel to remove the skin. I DO NOT recommend rinsing in running water to remove the skin. Water removes much of the flavor that you have been working so hard to create. After peeling, the chile may be carefully slit open on one side to remove the seeds before stuffing for chile rellenos; or the stem and seeds may be removed prior to chopping to use in salsa or to puree for a sauce or soup.

Wear surgical or rubber gloves when handling chiles to avoid burning your skin. Remember to wash your hands after peeling chiles; if you forget and touch yourself, you may regret it. A vinegar rinse followed by soap and warm water works well.

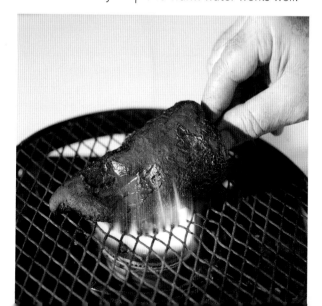

INGREDIENTS AND SUBSTITUTIONS

Use of the freshest and highest-quality ingredients is the first step in great cooking. Scrimping on quality will have a negative effect on the outcome of any recipe. Please try to get the very best that you can.

In the recipes that follow, I specify certain ingredients but often list alternative options. The recipes are written only as a guide. If a specific item is out of season, unavailable or you simply do not like it, make any substitution that suits your tastes. Real-life cooking is seldom exactly as it is depicted in books, so a good cook will adapt to the changing realities of an actual kitchen. Flexibility in use of ingredients also allows you to better express your own cooking style and flair.

The only ingredient that I am going to address specifically is salt. Salt helps bring out the flavors in foods and is very important in grilling. Just a little salt will make a big difference over no salt at all. The quality of the salt is very important. Typical iodized table salt contains a fair amount of impurities and does not flavor well. Kosher salt has a much higher purity standard and is the salt I use most often. There has been a proliferation of sea salts on the market recently. While these designer salts are certainly excellent, their level of quality over kosher salt often does not always correspond with the dramatically higher price. I do use sea salt when I am cooking something very special, or if I feel the need for a specific flavor.

NOTE: If you eliminate iodized salt from your diet, it is important, for health reasons, that you replace the iodine with another source.

Dry Rubs & Marinades

Dry rubs are, as the name implies, a mix of dried spices and seasonings that are applied to meat, seafood and some vegetables prior to grilling or smoking to add flavor, and in some cases to cure the meat. Essentially a marinade, dry rubs impart their flavors by combining with the natural juices and moistures or with any acids or oils that have been applied before the rub. The salt, and to some part the spices, help to cure meats by drawing out the blood and excess moisture in many meats. This space is then replaced by the dissolved flavors of the rub. The entire rub is not usually absorbed, however, and the remaining seasonings will form a flavorsome crust on the meat and help to retain the fats and moisture during the cooking process. I like to use dry rubs to season meats that will be accompanied with a sauce or salsa as the rub provides a good seasoning base while not overpowering the other tastes. Dry rubs are quicker to make and far less messy than wet marinades.

Any combination of dry spices can serve to make a rub, but there are some basics that will help you to make a personalized, custom flavor that is your own secret blend. Salt is almost always used, especially when a cure is desired; salt helps to bring out the natural flavors and enhances the taste of the other spices in the rub. A little sweetening with sugar will also bring out some richness and balance with hot spices like chiles. Sometimes a sweet taste is appropriate and other times you may not wish to taste the sweetness. Sugar, added in small amounts below the taste threshold for sweetness, will still have some flavor benefits. Brown sugar often tends to be too moist for dry rubs so, if you want that unrefined, full-flavored taste, raw or turbinado sugar works well. Fresh herbs and citrus peel may also be used but you will need to dry them thoroughly; either before combining in the rub or after the rub is assembled, carefully drying in a low oven to prevent burning.

Those of you that have attended my classes or have read my other cookbooks may wonder if you should toast the spices to enhance the flavor before combining in the rubs. If you are planning to use the entire rub, the same day that you make it, by all means, lightly toast the herbs, spices and chiles. If, however, you plan to keep some for later use, do not toast them, as toasted spices tend to lose their flavor quicker over time.

Dry rub ingredients

Adobos

ADOBO IS A GENERAL TERM for both wet and dry marinades, and sometimes sauces, in Spanish-speaking countries. Technically, all of the following recipes for dry rubs are adobos; however, I will address them separately and for my purposes here, adobo will refer to dry rubs that contain chiles.

RED CHILE Adobo

THIS IS A PERFECT WAY to add the flavors of New Mexico to grilled and roasted meats and game. I usually first brush the meat with something acidic like apple cider vinegar or lime and/or orange juice to help the rub adhere to the meat and to balance the chile flavor.

MAKES 2¼ CUPS

1 cup New Mexican red chile powder (I prefer the Chimayo variety), mild or medium-hot

½ cup kosher salt

¼ cup garlic powder

¼ cup onion powder

1 teaspoon ground cumin

1 tablespoon Mexican oregano, hand-rubbed fine

½ teaspoon ground coriander

½ teaspoon freshly ground black pepper

⅛ cup sugar

1. Mix all of the ingredients together.

2. Store airtight in a cool, dry place out of the sunlight.

ISLAND SPICE Adobo

THIS RUB HAS MOST OF THE FLAVORS of Jamaican jerk and can be used in place of the wet marinade; however, it does not contain the acids and Worcestershire sauce of the marinade and therefore will not tenderize the meat or give as intense a flavor.

MAKES ABOUT 1¾ CUPS

⅛ cup onion powder

⅛ cup granulated or powdered garlic

1 to 2 tablespoons cayenne pepper OR 1 to 2 teaspoons powdered habanero chile (be careful, this stuff is hot)

2 tablespoons mustard powder

1 tablespoon powdered ginger

1 tablespoon ground allspice

½ teaspoon ground coriander

1 teaspoon curry powder

1 tablespoon dried thyme, hand-rubbed fine

2 teaspoons dried orange peel, pulverized

1 teaspoon dried lime or lemon peel, pulverized

¼ cup raw or brown sugar

2 teaspoons black pepper

½ cup kosher salt

1. Mix all of the ingredients together.

2. Store airtight in a cool, dry place out of the sunlight.

SMOKY CHIPOTLE Adobo

THE MAGICAL SMOKY FLAVOR of chipotle chiles seems to make just about anything taste better. Chipotle chiles are red-ripened jalapeño chiles that have been smoked and dried for preservation. There is a lot of rich, deep flavor to go along with the concentrated heat of the chiles. This rub is versatile and is one of my favorites for grilled shrimp.

MAKES ABOUT 1½ CUPS

⅓ cup onion powder

⅛ cup granulated garlic or garlic powder

½ cup kosher or sea salt

1 teaspoon black pepper

2 teaspoons Mexican oregano, hand-rubbed fine

2 teaspoons granulated sugar

1 teaspoon paprika

¼ to ⅓ cup ground chipotle chile

1. Mix all of the ingredients together.

2. Store airtight in a cool, dry place out of the sunlight.

SEAFOOD Adobo

INTENDED FOR SEAFOOD, this adobo would also be good for chicken or pork. The brightness of the citrus zest adds an extra zing.

MAKES ABOUT 1⅛ CUPS

⅛ cup ground cayenne or New Mexico red chile powder

⅛ cup paprika

¼ cup onion powder

1 tablespoon granulated or powdered garlic

1 teaspoon ground coriander seed

½ teaspoon ground anise or allspice

2 tablespoons total: dried and pulverized citrus zest—lime, orange, lemon and/or grapefruit, any combination

1 teaspoon ground black pepper

1 teaspoon dried marjoram or thyme, hand-rubbed fine

1 tablespoon granulated sugar

¼ cup kosher or sea salt

1. Mix all of the ingredients together.

2. Store airtight in a cool, dry place out of the sunlight.

POULTRY Adobo

THIS DRY RUB, designed for grilled poultry, will work equally well for seasoning roasted or sautéed chicken, turkey, duck or quail. It could also be used as the seasoning in fried chicken! The main flavor is herbal with just a touch of chile heat.

MAKES ¾ CUP

2 teaspoons ancho chile powder

1 teaspoon ground chipotle chile or other hot chile powder

1 teaspoon paprika

¼ cup onion powder

⅛ cup granulated or powdered garlic

1 teaspoon dried rosemary, hand-rubbed fine

2 teaspoons dried sage, hand-rubbed fine

1 teaspoon dried thyme, marjoram or parsley, hand-rubbed fine

1 teaspoon mild curry powder

½ teaspoon ground cumin

3 tablespoons kosher or sea salt

1. Mix all of the ingredients together.

2. Store airtight in a cool, dry place out of the sunlight.

MEXICAN Adobo

THIS RUB CAPTURES the familiar essence of Mexican cuisine that was the flavor many North Americans were first introduced to in that style of cooking: "taco seasoning" or "chili powder," if you will. Although Mexican food has abundant variety and there is no one formula for the flavors, this adobo does capture an important taste combination from that style of cooking.

MAKES ABOUT 1⅓ CUPS

¼ cup ancho chile powder

⅛ cup guajillo, chipotle or New Mexican red chile powder

2 teaspoons Mexican oregano, hand-rubbed fine

2 teaspoons ground cumin

½ teaspoon ground coriander, optional

½ teaspoon cinnamon, optional

½ teaspoon ground allspice, optional

¼ cup onion powder

3 tablespoons granulated or powdered garlic

1 teaspoon granulated sugar

⅓ cup kosher or sea salt

1. Mix all of the ingredients together.

2. Store airtight in a cool, dry place out of the sunlight.

Mojo, Daniel's Famous All-Around Adobo sEasoNInG

THIS IS THE ONE that I always keep around my kitchen. We would be lost without it. It borrows from many of the other rubs listed here but is more universal. You can use it to season just about anything. In addition to a grill seasoning, I use it for meats and vegetables that are sautéed and for meats that are roasted. The recipe here is a large one, as we use a lot of it in my kitchen. You could make half or one-fourth of the quantity if you prefer.

MAKES ABOUT 2 ¾ CUPS

⅔ cup onion powder

⅓ cup granulated garlic or garlic powder

⅔ cup kosher or sea salt (coarse)

¼ to ⅓ cup raw sugar (turbinado)

2 tablespoons dried mustard

1 teaspoon ground allspice

¼ teaspoon ground cloves

1 teaspoon ground coriander

½ teaspoon ground cumin

1 tablespoon freshly ground black pepper

1 teaspoon dried thyme, hand-rubbed fine

1 teaspoon dried marjoram, hand-rubbed fine

2 teaspoons dried Mexican oregano, hand-rubbed fine

¼ cup paprika (Spanish smoked paprika works well)

⅛ cup dried chipotle chile powder

⅛ cup ancho chile powder

¼ to ½ cup New Mexico, California or guajillo red chile powder (mild or hot), depending on your taste

1. Mix all of the ingredients together.

2. Store airtight in a cool, dry place out of the sunlight.

Applying dry rub to brisket (see Smoked Spicy Beef Brisket on page 57).

SWEET SPICE Fruit rUb

YOU CAN USE THIS RUB to season fresh fruit like pineapple, apples or bananas for grilling or baking. After applying the rub, let the fruit sit a few minutes before cooking to allow the flavors to penetrate. Because of the sugar, you should be careful not to cook the fruit over too hot a flame or it will burn. The chile option adds a little extra spice and depth of flavor without much heat. This mixture makes a great pumpkin pie spice also.

MAKES ABOUT ¾ CUP

½ cup raw, white granulated or light brown sugar

3 tablespoons freshly ground canela (Mexican-style or Sri Lankan cinnamon)

2 teaspoons ground allspice

1 teaspoon ground cloves

½ teaspoon ground anise seeds

½ teaspoon ground ginger (optional)

1 teaspoon ancho chile (or other mild chile) powder (optional)

½ teaspoon salt

1. Mix all of the ingredients together.

2. Store airtight in a cool, dry place out of the sunlight.

CRACKED PEPPER-CORIANDER-LaveNdEr RuB

THE EXOTIC COMBINATION of the floral lavender, aromatic coriander, and the piquancy of the pepper in this rub are excellent for wild game or as a twist for grilled chicken or turkey. There is no salt in this recipe so you will need to salt the meat that you are using before applying the rub. If you lightly dry-toast the rub just before using it you will get more flavor.

MAKES ¾ CUP

¼ cup dried lavender flowers

¼ cup crushed coriander seeds

¼ cup cracked black peppercorns (I prefer the Tellicherry variety)

1. Mix all of the ingredients together.

2. Store airtight in a cool, dry place out of the sunlight.

Marinades

MARINADES ARE USED TO FLAVOR meats, poultry and seafood prior to cooking. They also help to tenderize many meats when left on them for extended periods of time. The moistness of a marinade allows it to penetrate the meat and often creates a deeper flavor than dry rubs. When grilling marinated items, it is important to remove the excess marinade to prevent burning.

ORANGE-ACHIOTE MaRiNaDe

THIS MARINADE IS REMINISCENT of the flavors of the Yucatan and Mayan Central America. The achiote is made from the seeds of the annatto tree that is native to those areas. It makes a great flavoring for seasoning grilled and smoked pork, chicken and turkey and it could also be used for seafood.

MAKES ABOUT 1 1/2 CUPS, ENOUGH FOR UP TO 4 POUNDS OF MEAT

1 teaspoon finely minced orange zest

1 cup orange juice

2 ounces prepared achiote paste

1 teaspoon ground allspice

2 teaspoons apple cider vinegar or rice vinegar

8 cloves garlic, roasted, peeled and chopped

2 teaspoons Mexican oregano, toasted and hand-rubbed fine OR 2 tablespoons fresh cilantro leaves

1/2 teaspoon ground black pepper

1 teaspoon salt

1 tablespoon vegetable oil

1/2 to 1 habanero chile, stemmed, seeded and chopped OR 1 to 2 teaspoons bottled habanero or Scotch bonnet pepper sauce

1. Combine all of the ingredients in a blender or food processor and puree until smooth.

2. Marinate the meat for at least 1 hour and up to overnight.

NOTE: *The chiles in this recipe are optional.*

Mexican Adobo Marinade

THE CLASSIC MEXICAN FLAVORING and marinade for meats that are to be grilled, smoked or roasted, this adobo also can be used for a sauce to serve after the meat is cooked. Just prepare the adobo with half of the vinegar, divide it in two parts and add the rest of the vinegar to the portion that is the marinade. To make the sauce, strain the other portion of the adobo into a hot skillet with 2 tablespoons oil, stir while frying for about 1 minute (be careful, the adobo will splatter) and then add water or broth to make a sauce consistency. Simmer for 10 to 15 minutes and serve.

MAKES ABOUT 1¾ CUPS, ENOUGH FOR 3 TO 6 POUNDS OF MEAT

2 to 3 dried ancho chiles

1 to 2 chipotle chiles in adobo OR 2 dried guajillo, or New Mexican chiles

6 to 8 cloves garlic, roasted, peeled and chopped

1 medium white onion, peeled, sliced in 3 or 4 rounds and grilled or pan roasted until well browned with a little charring around the edges, coarsely chopped

1 teaspoon Mexican oregano, toasted OR 1 teaspoon fresh thyme, oregano or marjoram leaves

½ teaspoon cumin seeds, toasted and ground

1 teaspoon canela (Mexican cinnamon) or allspice, ground

½ teaspoon black pepper, ground

Pinch of ground cloves

2 tablespoons apple cider or other mild vinegar (not wine vinegar)

1 teaspoon salt

Enough cool water to puree (usually 1 to 2 tablespoons)

2 cups boiling water to soak the chiles

1. Toast the dry chiles on a hot skillet or heavy pan until a little color and a few black spots develop. Remove from the pan and cool. Take out the stem, and remove the seeds, then place in the boiling water, turn off the heat and soak for 12 to 15 minutes. Remove the chiles from the water and proceed.

2. Place all the ingredients in a blender, *molcajete* (mortar and pestle) or food processor and blend until smooth. Add only enough water to facilitate the blending; you do not want to dilute the adobo.

3. Smear the marinade over the entire surface of the meat at least 1 hour and up to 24 hours prior to cooking.

NOTE: If the meat is very thick or has a fat layer covering it, you might want to pierce it with a sharp knife to allow the adobo to penetrate.

GARLIC, HERB & CUMIN MaRiNaDe

THIS RECIPE, while not containing chiles, lends a distinctively Latin American flavor to grilled meats, seafood and vegetables. It should be made fresh for each use, as it does not keep well.

MAKES ABOUT ¾ CUP, ENOUGH TO MARINATE UP TO 4 POUNDS

6 cloves garlic, peeled and minced

2 tablespoons fresh herb leaves, finely chopped (thyme, marjoram, oregano, rosemary, basil, sage, parsley, cilantro; any or all)

2 tablespoons red wine or Spanish sherry vinegar

1 tablespoon citrus juice

2 teaspoons whole cumin seeds, toasted

1 teaspoon ground or cracked black pepper

1 teaspoon kosher or sea salt

1 teaspoon Worcestershire or soy sauce

3 tablespoons olive oil

1. Mix all ingredients together and let sit for 10 to 15 minutes for the flavors to develop.

2. Spread evenly over the meat and marinate for 30 minutes to 2 hours before cooking.

LEMON-ANISE MaRiNaDe

THIS EASY MARINADE combines the tartness and scent of lemons with the natural sweetness and exotic aroma of anise. Anise and similarly scented herbs are used extensively throughout the Americas for both sweet and savory dishes. This marinade is excellent for delicately flavored grill items like scallops, fish and chicken. You could replace half of the lemon juice and zest with orange for a sweeter variation.

2 teaspoons finely minced lemon zest

2 tablespoons lemon juice

1 tablespoon + 1 teaspoon anise seeds, lightly toasted

1 teaspoon cracked black pepper

2 cloves garlic, minced

2 scallions (green onions), finely chopped

1 teaspoon salt

3 tablespoons olive oil

1 tablespoon chopped cilantro or parsley leaves (optional)

1. Mix all ingredients together and let sit for 10 to 15 minutes for the flavors to develop.

2. Spread evenly over the meat and marinate for 30 minutes to 2 hours before cooking.

Direct Grilling

Grilling over an open fire or coals most likely was developed shortly after humans first discovered how to tame fire itself. There is nothing like the taste that is achieved by cooking over flames and coals. The direct heat browns the meat and adds caramelized flavors and the smoke contributes a seductive acridity and richness. The use of natural fuels certainly develops the very best flavors; however, the convenience of gas grills and their accurate heat controls make them very appealing, and the result is still very good.

Whether you use natural fuels or gas, high-tech or simple equipment, the main goal of direct grilling is to use a fairly high heat to give your food that outdoorsy, rich smoky flavor and excellent color. It always takes careful attention to maintain that fine line between cooking too slowly and burning the food. There is no magic formula; practice makes perfect and the more you grill, the better you will get. The following recipes will help to guide you through some of the various approaches to direct grilling using different types of ingredients.

Lamb Chops Adovada (see page 26)

LAMB CHOPS AdovadA

CARNE ADOVADA is a tradition in New Mexican cooking that has its roots in the Mexican dish *Adobo Rojo*. It was a method used to preserve meats before refrigeration and freezers were available. A spicy mix of herbs, aromatic seeds and dried red chiles combined with vinegar helped keep the meat fresh for several weeks when stored in a cool place. The meat was then slow roasted in the marinade, resulting in stunning flavors. You may also use pork chops, pork tenderloin or venison in this recipe.

SERVES 6 TO 8

2 tablespoons vegetable oil

½ medium white onion, coarsely chopped

8 whole peeled garlic cloves

⅓ cup New Mexico pure red chile powder (mild or hot as desired), lightly toasted

1 teaspoon coriander seeds, lightly toasted

½ teaspoon cumin seeds, lightly toasted

½ teaspoon freshly ground black pepper

2 teaspoons all-purpose flour

2½ cups cool water

⅛ cup honey

2 teaspoons + 1 teaspoon salt

1 tablespoon + ¼ cup sherry or apple cider vinegar

2 tablespoons fresh oregano leaves OR 1 tablespoon toasted Mexican oregano

2 teaspoons ground canela (Mexican cinnamon)

½ teaspoon ground cloves or allspice

2 tablespoons chopped fresh cilantro leaves (optional)

2 tablespoons chile caribe (coarse New Mexican red chile flakes), optional

2 lamb racks cut into double chops OR 2 whole boneless lamb loin strips OR lamb T-bone steaks (about 4½ pounds)

1. Heat the oil in a sauté pan on medium high, add the onion and garlic cloves and cook until slightly browned. Add the chile powder, coriander, cumin, and black pepper and cook 1 more minute. Add the flour and cook another minute while stirring constantly.

2. Remove from heat and stir in the water, honey, 2 teaspoons salt, and 1 tablespoon vinegar. Add the oregano, canela, cloves or allspice, and optional cilantro and puree until smooth in a blender.

3. Strain with a medium sieve or china cap and divide the sauce in half.

4. In the first half, add the remaining vinegar and the optional chile caribe. Season the lamb with 1 teaspoon salt and place in a nonreactive container or a large plastic freezer bag along with this first half of the sauce. Marinate for at least 1 hour and up to overnight in the refrigerator.

5. Bring the remaining half of the sauce to a boil, then reduce heat to simmer and cook for 10 to 15 minutes; keep warm while the lamb is cooking.

6. Remove the lamb from the marinade and shake off excess. Cook directly on a medium-hot grill, turning to char all sides, until the desired doneness (medium-rare to medium is recommended). If using whole loin, carve into individual portions after resting.

7. Serve with some of the warmed sauce under the lamb.

CARNE ASADA TaMpiqUeña

A QUINTESSENTIAL MEXICAN FAVORITE served at high-end restaurants as well as at street stalls, the contemporary standard for Carne Asada was first presented by a Mexico City chef who originally hailed from Tampico; hence the title. The more expensive versions utilize beef tenderloin, and of course, you may prepare it that way; however, I think that the beauty of the dish lies in its simplicity and the full flavor of a less expensive cut of beef, sliced and pounded thin to make it tender. Carne Asada is cooked over an open flame, coals or on a flat griddle. To me there is no comparison; the smoky aroma that results from direct grilling is superior, but the dish can also be wonderful when cooked on a stovetop grill. Serve Carne Asada with an array of condiments, salsas and tortillas along with your favorite side dishes for a create-your-own feast. Grilled Scallions (see page 96) are the classic garnish for Carne Asada.

SERVES 4 TO 6

2 to 2½ pounds sirloin, chuck, round or beef tenderloin steak

Juice of 3 limes

2 tablespoons vegetable oil

2 to 3 tablespoons of your favorite dry rub (Smoky Chipotle Adobo, page 15, would be my choice) or salt and pepper to taste

1. Slice or butterfly the meat into sheets about ⅜ to ½ inch thick.

2. Place the meat between two sheets of plastic wrap and carefully pound it with a kitchen mallet, tenderizer or a heavy rolling pin until it is about ⅓ to ½ of the original thickness and uniform. *NOTE: Do not pound the meat if you are using tenderloin. It is too soft and might break apart. Just slice it thin.*

3. Sprinkle the lime juice evenly over the meat surface, wait 5 minutes and then brush with the oil.

4. Season with the dry rub or salt and pepper and then cover and put aside to marinate for 30 minutes to 1 hour.

5. Char grill the meat over high heat for about 3 to 4 minutes on the first side, turn over and cook for about 2 more minutes.

6. Allow to rest for about 5 minutes, then slice into thin strips or chop finely to serve.

"The Works" Burger

THIS IS MY TAKE on a past local favorite in northern New Mexico, where I live. It was served for years at the popular carryout restaurant, Lovato's, in Dixon. People were known to drive more than 30 miles to lunch on Lovato Burgers. Unfortunately, they have closed, so I was compelled to re-create it at home. The toppings are only suggestions; please feel free to garnish your burgers with anything that strikes your fancy.

SERVES 6

FOR THE BURGER

2½ to 3 pounds ground chuck or sirloin (anything less than 15 percent fat content gets a little too dry for char grilling)

1 to 1½ tablespoons Mojo, Smoky Chipotle or other dry rub (see pages 14–20)

FOR THE TOPPINGS

6 thick slices bacon

12 ¼-inch-thick slices portobello, shiitake or other large mushrooms

6 onion slices, ¼ to ⅜ inch thick

1 or 2 tablespoons olive oil

½ cup roasted, peeled, seeded and chopped New Mexico green chiles or poblano chiles (2 to 3 good-sized chiles)

Sliced or shredded cheese (provolone, cheddar, Swiss, smoked gouda, bleu cheese, etc.)

6 large hamburger buns

Mayonnaise

Mustard

1 large or 2 medium avocados, sliced OR ½ cup guacamole

Lettuce

Sliced tomatoes

1. Divide the ground beef into 6 equal portions and shape into patties about ¾-inch thick. Season the patties with the dry rub and set aside while the grill heats and you prepare the accompaniments.

2. Cook the bacon halfway. (The simplest method is to place the slices between two paper towels and microwave for 4 to 5 minutes.)

3. Lightly brush the mushroom and onion slices with oil and then season with dry rub or salt and pepper. Cook on the grill until well marked and the onions are tender.

4. Cook the bacon slices over low or indirect heat until done (beware of flare-ups caused by the fat dripping).

5. Cook the patties over direct heat, 5 to 6 minutes on the first side, then turn over and continue until desired doneness.

6. About 1 minute before the meat is done, top it with the chiles, bacon, onion, mushrooms, and cheese.

7. Toast the buns and dress with mayonnaise, mustard, avocado, lettuce, and tomatoes as desired. Add the burgers and toppings, and enjoy!

"The Works" Burger

ULTIMATE CHAR GRILLED StEaK
WITH MUSHROOMS, ROASTED CHILES & CARAMELIZED ONIONS

FOR MEAT LOVERS, there is nothing that can compare with a top-quality, thick, juicy steak cooked outdoors. Not much is required, a little seasoning, some wood chunks or chips to add smoky flavor and a simple sauce or salsa to top it. The following preparation is one of my favorites; I prepare it often at home; or for convenience I will make the topping and season the meat in advance to take along when camping or picnicking.

SERVES 4 TO 6

FOR THE STEAKS

4 to 6 strip loin, T-bone, or rib-eye steaks, around 1½ inches thick (dry aging produces some of the most flavorful, tender and juicy steaks)

2 teaspoons Worcestershire sauce

2 tablespoons good-quality olive oil

3 to 4 tablespoons Red Chile, Smoky Chipotle or Mojo dry rub (see pages 14, 15 and 18) or salt and pepper

2 sprigs per steak of fresh rosemary, thyme, sweet marjoram or oregano (optional)

Hardwood chunks or chips for smoke flavor

1. Spread the surface of the steaks with Worcestershire sauce and then spread with oil.

2. Sprinkle the dry rub or salt and pepper evenly over the surface of the steaks and, if using, press a sprig of the fresh herbs on each side of each steak.

3. Let sit at room temperature for 30 minutes. *NOTE: you may season the steaks up to 24 hours in advance and refrigerate. Temper the meat for 30 minutes before proceeding.*

4. Cook the steaks on a grill over medium-high heat until desired doneness. Use hardwood chunks or chips to add flavor. Rest before serving (see page 9).

(ingredients, recipe continued on page 32)

*Ultimate Char Grilled Steak with Mushrooms,
Roasted Chiles & Caramelized Onions*

(continued from page 30)

FOR THE TOPPING

2 tablespoons olive oil

½ cup shiitake, portobello or crimini mushrooms, sliced ¼ inch thick

1 tablespoon + 2 tablespoons butter

1 medium white or sweet yellow onion, peeled and cut in thin slivers

Salt to taste

2 medium poblano, New Mexican green or Anaheim chiles (or 1 chile and 1 sweet red pepper), fire-roasted, peeled, seeded and cut into ¼-inch-wide strips

Dash of Worcestershire sauce

Generous splash of red wine or sherry vinegar

Black pepper to taste

1 teaspoon fresh sweet marjoram or oregano leaves OR 1 teaspoon toasted dried Mexican oregano

5. In a preheated skillet or sauté pan, add the oil and sauté the mushrooms on high heat until browned around the edges, 2 to 3 minutes. Remove from pan.

6. Reduce the heat to medium-low; add 1 tablespoon butter, onion, and salt. Cover and cook, stirring occasionally, until the onion is golden brown and sweet, 10 to 12 minutes. Uncover for the last 5 minutes or so to dry out the extra moisture.

7. Increase the heat to medium-high, add the cooked mushrooms and the roasted chile strips and cook 1 more minute.

8. Add the Worcestershire sauce, vinegar, and black pepper and stir well. Taste for salt and adjust if needed.

9. Turn off the heat, add the herbs, and stir in the remaining butter until melted. Serve topping over steak immediately with a salsa of your choice on the side.

NOTE: If you make this sauce in advance, do not make the final addition of butter until you are ready to serve. Just reheat the sauce and then add the butter before you serve it.

Mexican Street Vendor–Style Hot dogS

MANY OF US ARE RELUCTANT to admit that we still crave the taste of a hot dog skewered on a stick and cooked over the campfire. After many years of abstaining from that childhood memory, I succumbed to the intoxicating aroma of char grilled hot dogs offered by a street vendor in the small town of Ascensión, Chihuahua, Mexico. All around Mexico, the hot dogs are served with an array of condiments and seasonings to complement the wieners. The hot dog is also usually wrapped in a slice of bacon to add more flavor while cooking. I have since become an enthusiastic client of many similar *comedores*, or food vendors, in that country. To share the treat with friends and family back home I developed this recipe. You could also use sausages (bratwurst, Italian, etc.) for this; adjust the cooking time accordingly. I hope that you enjoy it too.

SERVES 6 TO 8 (OR 4 WITH FULL-SIZE APPETITES)

1 large onion, peeled and thinly sliced

2 teaspoons vegetable oil

Dash of salt

8 slices bacon

8 quality hot dogs, franks or sausages

Toothpicks for securing the bacon

1 cup refried beans

8 hot dog buns or flour tortillas

¾ cup shredded or crumbled cheese (your favorite)

⅓ to ½ cup roasted, peeled and diced green chiles (New Mexico, poblano, Anaheim, jalapeño, etc.) or pickled, sliced jalapeño or serrano chiles

½ cup diced tomatoes

Mustard (optional)

1. Cook the onion in a skillet with the oil and salt until golden brown and aromatic.

2. Preheat your grill to medium.

3. Attach a slice of the bacon to one end of the hot dog with a toothpick. Snugly wrap the bacon around the dog in a spiral that completes at the other end and secure with another toothpick.

4. Heat the refried beans.

5. Slowly cook the hot dogs on the grill, turning occasionally, until the bacon is fully cooked and just beginning to crisp.

6. Toast the buns or tortillas over the grill, spread with some of the beans and place a hot dog in each.

7. Add the cheese, chiles, and tomatoes and if you like, the mustard. Enjoy.

NOTE: *For a tropical variation you could prepare the hot dogs "Hawaiian-style" by using Grilled Pineapple Salsa (see page 75) in place of the chiles, onions and tomatoes; with or without the beans.*

GAUCHO BeEfstEaK

WITH CHIMICHURRI

IN THE ARGENTINEAN PLAINS REGION called the Pampas, the *vaqueros*, or cowboys, are famous for their grilled beef. These simple preparations are usually cooked over an open fire and served with simple accompaniments. I have chosen Chimichurri, one of the most renowned salsas from that region. Please feel free to substitute your favorite cut of beefsteak: sirloin, rib-eye, strip steak, etc., in this recipe.

SERVES 6

3½ to 4 pounds trimmed flank steak

1 tablespoon olive or vegetable oil

⅛ to ¼ cup dry rub (Red Chile, Smoky Chipotle, Mexican Adobo or Mojo, see pages 14–20)

1 recipe Chimichurri (see page 85)

1. Coat the beef with the oil and then evenly apply the rub. Allow to sit for 5 to 10 minutes to absorb the rub.

2. Spread ¼ cup Chimichurri evenly over the meat and marinate at room temperature for 20 to 30 minutes.

3. Grill on high heat until well charred and cooked to your liking (rare to medium recommended). Remove from heat.

4. Rest the meat, loosely covered, for 10 to 15 minutes and then slice across the grain.

5. Serve with the remaining Chimichurri sauce.

Gaucho Beefsteak with Chimichurri

MANGO-HONEY PORK TENDERLOIN

THE SWEETNESS OF THE HONEY AND MANGO combined with the sharp heat of the serrano chile and the brightness of the cilantro make a perfect foil for grilled pork. This recipe can be completed in 30 minutes from start to finish and it will taste like you have slaved for hours in the kitchen. The pork is great with the sauce alone but a salsa like Charred Cherry or Pear Tomato Salsa (see page 77) or Tropical Fruit Salsa (see page 74) will complement the mango well. Serve with Grilled Plantain Tostones (see page 101) as shown at right. Pork chops or center-cut whole pork loin could also be used here; adjust the cooking times accordingly.

SERVES 4 TO 6

FOR THE PORK

2 to 3 whole pork tenderloins (about 2 to 2½ pounds), trimmed and silver skin removed

2 tablespoons mild vinegar or lime juice

2 tablespoons vegetable oil

1 to 2 tablespoons Mojo, Island Spice Adobo or other favorite dry rub (see pages 14–20)

FOR THE SAUCE

1 whole ripe mango, peeled, seeded and roughly chopped OR ⅔ cup frozen mango chunks

1 clove peeled garlic, crushed

1 or 2 serrano or habanero chiles, stemmed and roughly chopped (seed the habanero to help control the heat)

¼ cup honey

1 tablespoon soy sauce

½ teaspoon salt

1 tablespoon vegetable oil

2 tablespoons lime juice or mild vinegar

3 tablespoons cool water

2 tablespoons chopped cilantro leaves

1. Preheat your grill to medium.

2. Brush the pork with the vinegar then the oil.

3. Sprinkle with the dry rub and set aside.

4. Combine all of the sauce ingredients in a blender and puree until smooth. Divide the sauce into two equal parts.

5. Place the first half of the sauce in a saucepan and heat to boiling, then reduce heat to simmer for 10 minutes. Add more water as needed if sauce becomes too thick.

6. Quickly sear the pork on all sides over direct heat. Move the pork to a less direct spot on the grill or reduce the heat; brush the surface of the meat with some of the remaining, uncooked sauce.

7. Cook for a few minutes and repeat several more times to form a glaze on the tenderloin. Do not overcook; pork, especially tenderloin, tastes best when a little pink remains.

8. Rest the meat for a few minutes, then slice and serve with some of the heated sauce.

Mango-Honey Pork Tenderloin with Grilled Tostones

RED CHILE–APPLE CIDER GLAZED
PoRk chOps

I CAME UP WITH THIS RECIPE when I was the chef at a restaurant in Salt Lake City. I was homesick for New Mexico and wanted to recapture some of my favorite flavors from back home. Red chile, tart apples and juicy meat cooked over a fire seemed to cover it well. The sweet, sour, spicy and smoky flavors have a universal appeal whether you hail from New Mexico, London, or somewhere else. If you have a smoker, you may also first smoke the chops and then heat them on the grill or in a hot (400-degree) oven to cook on the glaze before serving.

SERVES 6 TO 8

4 to 5 pounds center-cut loin or rib pork chops, 3/4 to 1 1/2 inches thick (the number of chops will depend on their thickness)

Brine (see page 40)

1 to 2 tablespoons Red Chile Adobo or Mojo dry rub (see pages 14–20) OR salt and pepper

1/2 gallon apple cider or juice

3 tablespoons honey

1/8 cup sugar

4 cloves garlic

6 whole allspice berries, lightly toasted and cracked OR 1 tablespoon ground allspice

1 teaspoon coriander seeds, lightly toasted

2 bay leaves, toasted

4 whole cloves

1 stick canela (Mexican or Sri Lankan cinnamon)

1/2 teaspoon salt

1/4 cup toasted New Mexico red chile powder

3 tablespoons toasted ancho chile powder

1 tablespoon vegetable oil

1/4 cup apple cider vinegar

1. Place pork chops in the brine using a plate or other heavy object to keep meat immersed.

2. Refrigerate and leave meat in brine for at least 1 hour and up to 24 hours.

3. Drain the meat well and pat dry before cooking.

4. Season with the dry rub or salt and pepper.

5. Combine all remaining ingredients in a heavy saucepan to make the glaze; boil until reduced by two-thirds.

6. Strain to remove solid materials.

7. Continue cooking glaze at a lower heat, to avoid burning, until reduced by one-third more (should be the consistency of thick maple syrup).

8. Cook the chops on a grill, using wood chunks or chips for flavor, until desired doneness. Brush several times with the Red Chile–Apple Cider Glaze towards the end of the cooking process.

9. Use additional glaze as a sauce when plating and, if desired, top with Piñon Apple Chutney (see page 83) as shown at right.

*Red Chile–Apple Cider Glazed Pork Chops
with Piñon-Apple Chutney*

BriNE

THIS BASIC BRINE may be used for most meats before smoking or grilling. It is particularly effective with poultry followed by pork, seafood and beef. Brining imparts moisture and flavor and helps to tenderize, cure and preserve the meat. Generally, you should brine seafood for 20 to 30 minutes, poultry for 30 minutes up to 1½ hours and pork or beef anywhere from 1 to 24 hours, depending on the amount of curing you desire. Feel free to play around with the seasonings to suit you taste and the recipe that you are preparing.

MAKES ENOUGH FOR UP TO 5 POUNDS OF MEAT

6 cups cool water

⅛ cup kosher or sea salt

⅛ cup sugar

2 tablespoons apple cider vinegar

8 toasted whole peppercorns, cracked

8 toasted whole allspice berries, cracked

4 toasted bay leaves, crushed

1 stick canela (Mexican cinnamon), crushed

1. Combine all ingredients together in a nonreactive dish or pan.

OREGANO ChickeN

THIS IS A SIMPLE PREPARATION that shows the Mediterranean influence in Latin American cooking. Oregano chicken is often baked solely in the oven but the smoky, charred flavors of the grill are a nice complement to the herbs and garlic. If you have good control of your grill heat and are careful not to burn the chicken, you may skip the oven step and cook the chicken entirely on the grill. You may want to cook extra as the leftovers are excellent for chicken sandwiches, tacos or salads.

SERVES 4

1 whole chicken (2¼ to 2¾ pounds), quartered

1 to 2 tablespoons of your favorite dry rub (see pages 14–20) or salt and pepper to taste

6 cloves garlic, peeled

Juice of 1 lemon

¼ cup fresh oregano or sweet marjoram leaves OR 2 tablespoons toasted dried Mexican oregano

2 teaspoons full-flavored mustard

1 teaspoon salt

3 tablespoons olive oil

1 jalapeño chile, stemmed, seeded and minced (optional)

1. Rinse the chicken and pat dry. Season with the dry rub or salt and pepper and place in a baking dish or roasting pan.

2. Place in a preheated 375-degree oven and bake for 25 minutes.

3. Preheat your grill to medium.

4. Crush the remaining ingredients in a mortar and pestle or puree in a blender and pour over the pre-baked chicken to cover. Marinate for 10 to 15 minutes.

5. Cook on the grill until the skin is browned and slightly charred and the chicken is cooked through.

Raspberry-Chile Glazed Chicken Roulade

Filled with Roasted Poblano Chiles, Goat Cheese & Mushrooms

THESE ROULADES are simple, elegant and tasty with a striking presentation. They reflect a contemporary Southwestern approach to classic flavors. You may prepare them up to a day in advance and store wrapped in the refrigerator.

Serves 6

3 tablespoons olive oil

Dash of salt and pepper

1 cup oyster mushrooms, cleaned and sliced bite-sized

6 boneless, skinless chicken thighs (you may also use chicken breast but you must be careful not to dry it out when cooking; the dark meat retains more moisture and has a richer flavor)

1 to 2 teaspoons Poultry Adobo, Smoky Chipotle Adobo or Mojo dry rub (see pages 14–20) OR salt and pepper

6 ounces mild goat cheese, camembert or cream cheese

2 poblano, New Mexican green or Anaheim chiles, roasted, peeled, seeded and cut into ¼-inch-wide strips (sweet red peppers could also be used)

2 tablespoons fresh marjoram or oregano leaves (optional)

Bamboo skewers or toothpicks to secure the roulades

1 6-ounce jar red chile-raspberry jam or jelly, heated and strained of seeds

NOTE: *To make your own jam, simply combine a jar of raspberry jam or jelly with 1 to 2 teaspoons lightly toasted New Mexican red chile powder OR ½ to 1 teaspoon chipotle chile powder and simmer in a saucepan for 8 to 10 minutes.*

1. Heat the oil in a heavy skillet; add salt and pepper and the mushrooms and sauté on high heat until nicely browned. Remove the mushrooms and reserve.

2. Trim the chicken thighs of excess fat and any irregular edges. Place each thigh between two pieces of plastic wrap on a cutting board or smooth countertop. Gently pound the meat with a kitchen mallet to a uniform ¼-inch thickness. You should end up with a rectangle that is roughly 6 x 3 ½- to 4-inches wide.

3. Season each piece with the dry rub or salt and pepper. Divide the cheese into equal parts and spread on the inside of each thigh (the skin side is the outside) to cover the center ⅓ to ½ of the meat.

4. Place ⅙ of the chile strips and then ⅙ of the mushrooms on top of the cheese on each piece. If using, sprinkle some of the marjoram or oregano on top.

5. Roll each piece into long cylinders, tucking in about ¾ of an inch of each end halfway through the rolling to seal. Secure the seam with a skewer or toothpick.

6. Grill over direct heat, turning often, until the entire surface is well marked and colored.

7. Move the roulades to indirect grill heat or place in a 350-degree oven. Brush half of the jam over each one and cook for a few minutes more to set the glaze.

8. After removing from the heat, let rest, loosely covered, for 4 to 5 minutes; remove skewers or toothpicks.

9. Slice into several pieces and drizzle with the remaining warm jam to serve.

Raspberry-Chile Glazed Chicken Roulade

EASY JERK-SEASONED GRILLED Chicken QuArTeRs

THIS RECIPE PROVIDES a quicker and easier alternative to jerk, the famous method of cooking pork and chicken in the Caribbean islands. It is not purely authentic; however, the results are tasty. Try serving with Coconut Curried Rice and Black-Eyed Peas (see page 106) as shown at right.

SERVES 6 TO 8

2 tablespoons Worcestershire sauce

Juice of 1 lime

Juice of 1 orange

1 teaspoon prepared yellow mustard

1 tablespoon vegetable oil

2 whole chickens (2¼ to 2½ pounds each), quartered or the equivalent in cut up chicken pieces

3 to 4 tablespoons Island Spice Adobo dry rub (see page 15)

1. Combine the Worcestershire, lime and orange juices with the mustard and oil, then toss the chicken in this mixture to coat evenly.

2. Sprinkle the chicken pieces with the dry rub and then cover and marinate in the refrigerator for 1 to 2 hours.

3. Place in a baking dish or roaster pan and bake in a preheated 375-degree oven for 20 minutes.

4. Preheat your grill.

5. Grill the chicken pieces over medium heat until evenly browned and cooked through.

Easy Jerk-Seasoned Grilled Chicken Quarters with Coconut Curried Rice and Black-Eyed Peas

TUNA STEAKS
WITH ACHIOTE CITRUS GLAZE

THIS IS A QUICK AND STRAIGHTFORWARD preparation that adds color and flavor to fresh fish on the grill. Achiote paste is made from the seeds of the annatto tree that is native to Mexico, Central America and the Caribbean and is used extensively in the cooking of those areas. It imparts a deep red color and a rich earthy flavor to seafood, poultry and meat. Tuna is my favorite for this recipe, but the glaze works great on any fresh fish. When the weather is cold or you just do not have time, an indoor grill also may be used for a summer-like result that is delicious and also low in fat. Serve with Tropical Fruit Salsa, Cilantro-Pumpkinseed Pesto or Grilled Pineapple Salsa (see pages 74, 75 and 82) or simply a squeeze of fresh lime juice.

SERVES 4 TO 6

3 tablespoons achiote seasoning paste (available in Mexican, Latin-American and specialty food markets)

1 teaspoon orange zest

1 teaspoon lime zest

Juice of 1 lime and 1 orange

2 cloves peeled garlic

1 tablespoon fresh cilantro or oregano

½ teaspoon ground allspice

½ teaspoon black pepper

1 teaspoon salt

1 tablespoon honey or brown sugar

1 teaspoon habanero hot sauce or your favorite other hot sauce (optional)

2 tablespoons vegetable oil

4 to 6 fresh tuna steaks (5 to 7 ounces each) ¾ to 1 inch thick, or the fish of your choice

1. Place all ingredients except the fish in a blender or food processor and puree until smooth. Reserve ⅓ of the glaze for basting during cooking.

2. Coat the fish with ⅔ of the glaze and marinate for 10 to 30 minutes.

3. Cook on a preheated grill over fairly high direct heat for about 3 to 4 minutes, turn and cook for another 2 to 3 minutes, basting with the remaining glaze several times (do not overcook, tuna should still be pink in the middle). For a rare tuna, decrease the cooking time by 1 to 1½ minutes per side.

Tuna Steaks with Achiote Citrus Glaze served with Tropical Fruit Salsa

LIME-MARINATED SPICY GriLLed SaLmOn

THIS IS AN UNCOMPLICATED and tasty way to cook this popular fish. The natural oiliness of salmon is perfect for grilling and the citrus along with the spice rub adds an intensity that contrasts well with the salmon's richness.

SERVES 6

2½-pound salmon fillet, skinned and pin bones removed

¼ to ⅓ cup freshly squeezed lime juice

2 teaspoons finely chopped lime zest

3 cloves garlic, crushed

2 tablespoons finely chopped cilantro (optional)

2 to 3 tablespoons Smoky Chipotle, Mojo or Red Chile or other dry rub (see pages 14–20)

⅛ cup vegetable oil or cooking spray

1. Cut the salmon fillet into serving-sized portions (6 to 7 ounces each).

2. Preheat your grill to medium-high.

3. Combine the lime juice, zest, garlic and optional cilantro in a bowl and set aside for 10 to 15 minutes.

4. Brush or drizzle the salmon with the lime mixture to completely coat. Let sit for 5 minutes to absorb the flavor and to slightly dry.

5. Sprinkle the salmon evenly with the dry rub and let sit for 5 to 10 minutes more.

6. Brush the surface of the fish with the oil or spray to evenly coat.

7. Cook on the grill until done but still moist and not overcooked. The time will depend on the thickness of the fillets and the grill temperature.

NOTE: This recipe is perfect with Gazpacho Vegetable Salsa (see page 81), Grilled Pineapple Salsa (see page 75) or Cilantro-Pumpkinseed Pesto (see page 82).

*Lime-Marinated, Spicy Grilled Salmon
served with Cilantro-Pumpkinseed Pesto*

GRILLED CRAB ReLLenOs
WITH FIRE-ROASTED TOMATO SAUCE

CHILE RELLENOS NORTH of the border are usually filled with meat or cheese, batter-dipped, then fried; however, in Mexico they have a variety of fillings and are not always fried. Here I have filled the chiles with crab and cream cheese and they are heated through on the grill. The fire-roasted tomato sauce is the perfect complement to these tasty treats. If you use smaller chiles, the rellenos could also be served as an appetizer or first course.

SERVES 6 AS A MAIN COURSE OR UP TO 12 AS AN APPETIZER

12 ounces cream cheese, room temperature

2 ounces crumbled Cotija or feta cheese (optional)

2 to 3 tablespoons milk or half-and-half

1 to 1½ pounds lump crab-meat (I prefer blue or stone crab for this)

3 small scallions, finely chopped

¼ cup chopped cilantro

½ teaspoon salt

½ teaspoon black pepper

1 tablespoon lime juice

6 medium poblano chiles, roasted, peeled and carefully seeded so the chile remains intact with the stem still in place (see Techniques page 11)

FIRE-ROASTED TOMATO SAUCE

8 to 10 ripe Roma tomatoes (about 1½ pounds)

1 medium white onion, peeled and cut into thick, round slices

10 cloves garlic, peeled

1 small piece of foil, about 6 inches square

1 tablespoon Mexican oregano, toasted OR 3 to 4 leaves fresh epazote

1 habanero chile, charred, stemmed and seeded OR 2 to 3 chipotle chiles in adobo

1 tablespoon apple cider vinegar or rice vinegar

Generous pinch of ground cloves or allspice (optional)

1 teaspoon salt

2 tablespoons vegetable oil

Water as needed

1. Mix the cheeses with the milk until smooth. Mix the crab, scallions, cilantro, salt, and pepper and sprinkle with the lime juice. Combine the crab mixture with the cheese mixture and gently mix thoroughly.

2. Place enough of the crab mixture in each chile to fill about ⅔ full. Close the seam on the chile and gently squeeze to shape the relleno and evenly distribute the filling. Refrigerate until ready to grill.

3. To make the sauce, place the tomatoes along with the onion slices on a hot grill and char, turning occasionally until they are mostly blackened. Place the garlic on the foil and put on the grill at the same time as the tomatoes. Roast, turning once or twice, until the garlic is browned (almost black) in spots.

4. Preheat a heavy Dutch oven or skillet to medium high.

5. Place all of the sauce ingredients except the oil and water in a blender and puree until smooth.

6. Place the oil in the hot skillet and immediately strain the sauce into the oil. Fry, stirring constantly, for about 2 minutes. Reduce the heat and simmer for 20 minutes, adding water as needed to maintain a sauce consistency.

7. Cook the stuffed chiles on a medium-hot grill, turning occasionally until heated through, about 15 minutes. Spread the sauce in a platter or serving dish and arrange the chiles on top.

GRILLED HABANERO LOBSTER TAILS

I FIRST SAW THIS DISH PREPARED while having lunch with my family on the island of Cozumel off the Caribbean coast of Mexico. We were at a small, open-air *palapa*, or thatched-roof, restaurant on a remote part of the island. While we were eating, a small dive boat landed on the beach and after the divers had unloaded, the captain emerged with about a half dozen live lobsters that they had presumably caught while diving. He brought them to the kitchen and after a short negotiation, he began to prepare the lobsters. The recipe was simple; the lobsters were split in half lengthwise, sprinkled with fresh lime juice, rubbed with garlic and a split habanero chile. Salt and pepper were then added and the lobsters were cooked over a small grate over an open fire. Judging by the reactions of the dive group, the lobster was as delicious as it looked. Upon returning home, I was compelled to reproduce that recipe and this is the result.

SERVES 6

1 or 2 habanero chiles, stemmed, seeded and minced

2 cloves garlic, minced

3 tablespoons lime juice

1 teaspoon honey

Dash of cider vinegar

⅛ cup chopped cilantro (optional)

3 tablespoons olive or vegetable oil

6 lobster tails (7 to 9 ounces each), split in half lengthwise and vein removed

Salt and pepper

1. Combine the chiles, garlic, lime juice, honey, vinegar, and cilantro, if using.

2. Add the oil and mix well.

3. Brush the lobster with the mixture to coat well, then season with salt and pepper.

4. Grill over medium-high heat shell-side first for 4 to 5 minutes. Invert and continue cooking for 3 to 4 minutes, or until the lobster is just cooked through. (Be careful not to overcook.) Serve immediately.

NOTE: *You could also use whole split lobsters, ½ per guest.*

TAMARIND-GLAZED SUGARCANE
FiSH SkEWErS

TAMARIND IS ONE of the only spices thought to have originated in Africa. It was brought to India in ancient times and was introduced to the New World shortly after the Spanish conquest. Today it is grown and used extensively in Latin America, both for cooking and most importantly, in beverages. The concentrated sweetness and sourness of the tamarind balance the spiciness of the chipotle chiles on the fish. Using sugarcane skewers will add some sweetness and flavor and helps to create a sexy presentation; however, if you do not have any, you may use wooden or bamboo ones instead for excellent results. Shrimp or scallops may be used, all or in part, as a substitute for the fish.

SERVES 6

12 sugarcane skewers (available in Asian and Latin-American markets and some supermarkets and specialty food shops)

Water for soaking the skewers

2½ to 3 pounds fresh fish, cut into 1-inch chunks

2 tablespoons + 1 tablespoon vegetable oil

2 to 3 tablespoons Smoky Chipotle Adobo (see page 15)

¼ cup brown sugar

3 tablespoons hot water

6 tablespoons tamarind paste (available in Asian and Latin-American markets and specialty food shops)

1 tablespoon apple cider vinegar

2 tablespoons soy sauce

1 tablespoon bottled hot sauce (optional)

½ teaspoon salt

Chopped cilantro for garnish

1. Soak the skewers in water to help prevent burning.

2. Toss the fish chunks in 2 tablespoons of the oil and lay four at a time parallel on a cutting board or countertop. Pierce all four fish chunks with a skewer. The fish should be spaced so that they are close but not touching each other. Repeat until you have 12 skewers and have used all the fish.

3. Sprinkle with dry rub evenly and set aside.

4. Preheat your grill to medium-high.

5. Dissolve the brown sugar in the hot water, mix in the remaining ingredients, except cilantro, and stir until the tamarind is blended in smoothly.

6. Quickly sear the skewers on both sides on the grill and then begin brushing the tamarind glaze on the fish to coat. Continue cooking while brushing several times and turning the skewers until the glaze has begun to caramelize and the fish is cooked through.

7. Sprinkle with the cilantro to garnish.

NOTE: Bell peppers, pineapple, onions, tomatoes, chiles, or mushrooms, cut into 1-inch pieces, add great color and flavor to these skewers. Just alternate fish and vegetables as shown on page 53.

*Tamarind-Glazed
Sugarcane Fish Skewers*

Duck Breast
with Ancho Chile–Dried Cherry Sauce

THE EXOTIC AROMATICS of the dry rub perfume the duck meat while the earthy sweetness and mild heat of the sauce complement its richness. Dried cranberries could be used in place of the cherries.

Serves 6

FOR THE DUCK

6 small to medium or 3 large boneless, skin-on, duck breasts

1 teaspoon coarse salt

4 tablespoons Cracked Pepper-Coriander-Lavender Rub (see page 20)

FOR THE SAUCE

1 cup (about 4 ounces) dried cherries

1 cup red wine (Pinot Noir or Zinfandel work well)

2 tablespoons olive oil

6 to 8 small garlic cloves, peeled

1 to 2 ancho chiles, stemmed, seeded and cut into small (1 x ⅛-inch) strips

2 cups duck or chicken stock

Salt to taste

3 tablespoons butter (optional)

1. Rinse the duck in cold water and pat dry with a paper towel.

2. Score the fat, just through to the meat, in a criss-cross grid pattern about ½ inch wide.

3. Salt the meat and then evenly coat with dry rub; set aside at room temperature while preparing the sauce.

4. To make the sauce, soak the cherries in the wine.

5. Preheat your grill to medium-low. Heat a saucepan to medium-low and add the oil.

6. Add the garlic cloves and cook, stirring occasionally, until lightly browned.

7. Raise the temperature to medium-high and add the chile strips. Sauté while stirring until the aroma of the chiles is released (about 2 to 3 minutes).

8. Add the wine and cherries and reduce until most of the liquid is gone. Add the stock and cook until reduced by two-thirds. Taste and adjust for salt if needed. If using butter, stir into the sauce over heat to enrich and thicken just before serving.

9. Cook the duck breasts skin side down on the grill over medium-low heat or with indirect heat until most of the fat is rendered and the skin has begun to crisp (10 to 14 minutes).

10. Turn the breasts over and cook to desired done-ness (medium-rare to medium is perfect for duck, overcooking causes it to dry out and get tough).

11. Remove the duck from the grill, allow it to rest in a warm place for 5 to 8 minutes and slice. Pour some of the sauce over the sliced duck to serve.

SMOKING

SMOKING IS A METHOD of preserving and cooking meats that started in the New World. In the United States, we often associate smoking with barbeque, which is known as a specialty of the South, but its roots spring from the Caribbean and the name is tantalizingly similar to the barbacoa of Mexico. The jerk of the Caribbean islands seems to epitomize the origins of barbeque and the method likely spread through the slave trade and it was adapted in the various regions where it landed. Barbeque is truly an example of fusion cuisine.

Legends abound as to the origin of jerk; the most plausible attribute it to the method of preparing and preserving meat that was taught to the pirates or buccaneers that frequented the area by the Carib and Arawak Indians. On the islands of Hispaniola and Cuba, there were wild pigs that had established themselves after being brought to the New World by the Spanish. The islands were a great place to hide out and often the wild pigs were hunted for food. The meat was cut into thin sheets, seasoned with the indigenous allspice berries and local herbs and chiles and cooked over a fire made from the wood of the allspice or pimento tree. This method helped to preserve the meat and the results resembled bacon, or *boucan*, as it is in French; hence the term Buccaneers. In Jamaica, the Maroons, escaped slaves from West Africa, added the ginger brought in from Asia and the mustard and Worcestershire sauce from England and perfected the dish. The term jerk is most likely derived from the Spanish word *charqui*, where the word jerky also originated. It also seems to describe the method of pulling the meat apart for serving after it is ready.

Smoked Spicy Beef Brisket

Smoked Spicy Beef Brisket
with Chipotle Barbecue Sauce

WHILE NOT PRECISELY a Latin American dish, barbecued brisket is enjoyed throughout the Southwest and this recipe borrows from the flavors of Texas and Mexico. It seems like a lot of meat, but it will shrink quite a bit and you'll also want leftovers. I prefer oak or alder as the wood for smoking but you can also use mesquite for a stronger flavor.

SERVES 8 TO 10

FOR THE BRISKET

1 whole beef brisket (10 to 12 pounds)

¼ cup Worcestershire sauce

2 tablespoons cider vinegar

*¼ to ⅓ cup Smoky Chipotle (see page 15) mixed with
   1 tablespoon dried mustard OR Mojo Rub (see page 18)*

⅛ cup light brown sugar

FOR THE BBQ SAUCE *(MAKES ABOUT 3 CUPS)*

1 medium white onion, peeled and sliced

10 to 12 cloves garlic, peeled

⅛ cup apple cider vinegar

2 to 4 whole chipotle chiles in adobo (more if you like it hot)

2½ cups ketchup

1 tablespoon vegetable oil

¼ cup Worcestershire sauce

3 tablespoons prepared mustard

½ teaspoon ground cumin, toasted

1 teaspoon ground black pepper

1½ teaspoons salt

¾ cup beef broth or water

⅓ to ½ cup light brown sugar

1. Score the fat side of the brisket with a sharp knife in a crisscross pattern 2 inches apart, cutting into the meat below the fat about ½ inch deep.

2. Mix the Worcestershire sauce and the vinegar together and brush all over the surface of the meat.

3. Combine the dry rub and brown sugar. Sprinkle mixture evenly over the meat, taking care to get some in each of the cuts (see photo on page 19).

4. Wrap, bag, or cover tightly in a pan and marinate overnight in the refrigerator.

5. Unwrap the meat and place fat side up in a preheated smoker or covered grill set up for smoking. Place a pan under the meat to catch the fat drippings; baste the brisket with the drippings about every 30 to 45 minutes. Cook for 6½ to 8 hours at 275 to 300 degrees, or until the meat is fall-apart tender. Rest brisket for 10 to 15 minutes and then slice to serve.

6. To make the sauce, sauté the onion and garlic cloves in a preheated skillet until well browned. Place in a blender with the vinegar, chiles and ½ cup of the ketchup; puree until smooth.

7. Heat all of the ingredients, except the sugar, to boiling in a saucepan, then reduce to a simmer and cook for 45 minutes.

8. Add the sugar and continue cooking for 20 to 30 minutes until the desired thickness is attained.

9. Serve the brisket with warm BBQ sauce.

Smoked Leg of Lamb biRria

BIRRIA IS A METHOD of preparing mutton or goat and sometimes pork or beef. It is typically seasoned with a paste of chiles and spices and slow-cooked in an oven or steamer. My method of using the smoker lends an interesting note to the flavors. An excellent meat for tacos and a range of condiments, birria also stands alone as an elegant main course that would go well with Jicama Fiesta Slaw (see page 86) and Potatoes and Chiles Baked with Garlic and Sour Cream Sauce (see page 108).

SERVES 6 TO 8 OR MORE IF USING FOR TACOS

FOR THE LAMB

1 boneless leg of lamb, 4½ to 5½ pounds, with fat cap intact (you may use bone in lamb too, add 40 to 70 minutes to the smoking time)

Mexican Adobo Marinade (see page 22)

1. At least 2 hours in advance and preferably the day before, make 8 to 10, 2-inch incisions, 1 inch deep, evenly spaced over the surface of the lamb.

2. Rub the surface of the leg with the marinade (make sure that you press some into each incision, you may want to wear rubber gloves for this).

3. Cover and refrigerate until 1 hour before smoking.

4. Start your smoker and have the wood chunks or chips ready.

5. Take a piece of foil large enough to hold the lamb leg and arrange it in the smoker so that it will catch some of the cooking juices. Place the lamb on the foil, replace any marinade that has fallen off, and loosely cover with another piece of foil.

6. Smoke for 4½ to 6 hours at 300 to 325 degrees, until the meat is fork tender. Remove lamb from the smoker and rest for 15 minutes.

7. Slice the meat and serve with some sauce on top or shred it for tacos and mix part of the sauce in and serve the rest on the side.

FOR THE SAUCE

1 pound roma tomatoes

2 slices onion, ⅜ inch thick

8 cloves garlic, peeled

1 or 2 chipotle chiles in adobo

1 tablespoon apple cider or other mild vinegar

¼ to ⅓ cup water

2 tablespoons vegetable oil

2 teaspoons Mexican oregano, toasted and hand-rubbed fine OR 2 tablespoons chopped cilantro

½ teaspoon cumin seed, toasted and ground

1 teaspoon salt

Generous pinch of ground cloves

½ cup defatted cooking juices from the lamb

1. Place the tomatoes, onion, and garlic cloves on the foil with the lamb and smoke for about 1¼ hours.

2. When the lamb is done, puree the tomatoes, onions, garlic, chile, and vinegar in a blender with just enough water to facilitate.

3. In a preheated heavy skillet or Dutch oven, add the oil, and then strain the tomato mixture into the pan. Fry for about 2 minutes, stirring constantly, add the oregano, cumin, salt, cloves, and enough of the cooking juices and water, if needed, to give a medium-thick consistency of sauce.

4. Simmer for 10 minutes and serve hot.

JERKED PORK, IsLaNd StylE

IN THE CARIBBEAN ISLANDS, most notably in Jamaica, the smoky aroma of spicy island-style barbecue wafts from the many "jerk shacks" that are prevalent along the country roads and in the towns and villages. Jerk is a method of preparing pork and chicken that has developed over centuries and uses the native herbs and spices, some ingredients brought in by the European settlers and the Scotch bonnet or habanero chile for added zing.

This recipe calls for pork but it is also a popular method for chicken, in which case you will want to reduce the cooking time or use the recipe for Jerk-Seasoned Grilled Chicken Quarters (see page 44). Jerk is usually served with Scotch Bonnet Sauce (recipe on opposite) and several side dishes like Coconut Curried Rice and Black-Eyed Pea Salad (see page 106) or Fire-Roasted Corn Flan (see page 104).

SERVES 6 TO 8

4 to 5 pounds pork Boston butt or spare ribs

8 cloves garlic, peeled

½ bunch scallions or 1 small, peeled white onion, roughly chopped

1 inch peeled, fresh ginger, minced OR 2 teaspoons ground ginger

2 tablespoons fresh or dried thyme leaves

¼ cup fresh cilantro, roughly chopped

1 teaspoon lime zest (rind), minced

1 teaspoon orange zest, minced (optional)

Juice of 3 limes, about ¼ cup

Juice of 1 orange, about ¼ cup (optional)

2 tablespoons apple cider vinegar

2 tablespoons soy sauce

⅓ cup Worcestershire sauce

¼ cup prepared yellow mustard (the hot dog type, not the premium mustards)

⅓ cup brown sugar OR ¼ cup molasses

3 tablespoons dark rum (optional)

1 to 2 fresh Scotch bonnet or habanero chiles, rough chopped OR 2 to 3 tablespoons bottled Caribbean or other favorite hot sauce

2 tablespoons ground allspice

2 teaspoons ground black pepper

2 teaspoons salt

3 tablespoons vegetable oil

1. Cut the meat into portion-sized chunks.

2. Place all of the remaining ingredients in a blender or food processor and puree until smooth.

3. Put the meat in a large plastic bag or a nonreactive bowl and cover with the marinade. Seal and place in the refrigerator to marinate at least 2 hours or overnight, which is the best option.

4. Place in a smoker or on a covered grill away from the direct heat and slowly cook (325 degrees), turning occasionally, until the meat is tender, about 3½ to 4 hours.

5. Serve with Scotch Bonnet Chile Sauce or Fruit Salsa (see page 72).

SCOTCH BONNET CHILE SAUCE

BEWARE, THIS STUFF IS HOT. It has a lot of flavor, and a little goes a long way. You may keep this for about a week in your refrigerator.

MAKES ABOUT 1 CUP

1 or 2 Scotch bonnet or habanero chiles, stemmed, seeded and roughly chopped

2 tablespoons key lime juice (regular lime juice may be substituted)

1 teaspoon cider or rice vinegar

1 teaspoon sugar or honey

1 clove garlic, minced

½ teaspoon salt

⅔ cup cool water

1 scallion, thinly sliced

1 tablespoon chopped cilantro (optional)

1. Place all but the scallions and cilantro in a blender or food processor and puree until smooth.

2. Stir in the scallion slices and the cilantro, allow to sit a few minutes to mingle the flavors, and serve over grilled or smoked meats.

Cochinita Pibil

PORK WRAPPED IN BANANA LEAVES AND BAKED IN A PIT

Pibil is the Mayan word for a pit that is dug in the ground and then lined with stones to roast a suckling pig. A fire is built and allowed to burn for several hours until it has been reduced to smoldering coals. Meanwhile, the cochinita, or little pig, has been seasoned and marinated with the exotic flavors of the brick-red achiote, the bright taste of citrus and the floral heat of the habanero chile. Wrapped in banana leaves, the meat is placed in the pit, covered with the rocks and some palm leaves or wet burlap, and slow roasted overnight. This feast is then served family-style with fresh handmade tortillas, salsas, condiments, and lettuce to make your own tacos.

Although the banana leaves lend a distinct flavor to the meat as well as a dramatic presentation, a package of aluminum foil instead of the leaves also produces an outstanding dish.

ENOUGH COOKED PORK FOR 6 MAIN COURSE SERVINGS OR 30 TO 36 TACOS

1 package (1 pound) frozen banana leaves (available at specialty food stores and Latin American or Asian grocers) OR heavy-duty aluminum foil

1 medium, boneless pork butt or arm roast (5½ to 7½ pounds), trimmed but with some fat remaining

3 ounces achiote paste

12 cloves peeled garlic

1 medium white onion, coarsely chopped (¾ cup)

2 tablespoons allspice berries, toasted and cracked OR 1 tablespoon ground allspice

2 tablespoons Mexican oregano, toasted

1 teaspoon cumin seed, toasted and crushed

2 teaspoons cracked black pepper

6 bay leaves, toasted

2 tablespoons Worcestershire sauce (optional—not traditional, but I did learn the trick in Mexico)

Juice of 2 limes

Juice of 1 orange

¼ cup apple cider, pineapple or rice vinegar

2 to 3 fresh habanero or Scotch bonnet chiles, stems and seeds removed OR 2 to 3 tablespoons bottled habanero chile sauce

2 tablespoons vegetable oil

2 tablespoons salt

1. Thaw the banana leaves and rinse them well in cool water. Tear 8 ½-inch-wide strips off one leaf and tie two together to make a total of four strips to use later for ties. Or you can use heavy-duty aluminum foil if banana leaves are not available.

Step 2

2. Make several 1-inch-deep cuts on the fat side of the pork to allow the marinade to penetrate. Place the meat in a freezer bag or other large plastic bag or a large nonreactive container.

(continued on page 64)

Cochinita Pibil Feast

Step 3

Step 5

Step 7

Step 8

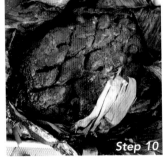
Step 10

(continued from page 62)

3. Mix all the other ingredients, except banana leaves, in a blender or food processor. Pour in with the pork, seal bag, and distribute well to coat the meat. Marinate at least 2 hours or overnight in the refrigerator.

4. Preheat smoker to 325 degrees.

5. Toast the banana leaves over direct heat to make them more pliable. Line the bottom of a heavy roasting pan with 2 or 3 of the banana leaves. They should overlap the pan on all sides.

6. Remove the pork roast from the bag and reserve the marinade.

7. Place pork fat side up on banana leaves in the pan. Pour about ½ cup of the marinade over top of the meat.

8. Place 3 or 4 more leaves over the pork and inside the bottom leaves. Pull bottom leaves around the meat; tie strips of banana leaves around this package from both directions to secure.

9. Smoke at 275 to 300 degrees for 5½ to 7 hours until meat is fork tender. Leaves will be darkened on the outside when finished and the internal temperature should be at least 185 degrees.

10. Allow to cool for 20 minutes and then slit banana leaves open with a sharp knife or scissors (be careful of the steam) and remove the pork or present on the leaves.

NOTE: *You may also prepare this in a covered grill. Place the wrapped pork in the grill away from the direct heat and smoke for 1½ hours, transfer to a 335-degree oven and bake for 3 to 4 hours until done.*

Smoked MarLin

SMOKED SEAFOOD is great for an appetizer, in salads or as a main course. Smoking increases the shelf life of fresh seafood as it preserves it. In Mazatlan, Mexico, smoked marlin is often shredded and used as a filling for empanadas (pastry turnovers) and to top tostadas or simply sliced and garnished with a flavorful salsa as an appetizer. You may substitute many varieties of fish or shellfish in this recipe.

1 piece fresh marlin loin (3 to 3½ pounds), skin removed

Juice of 1 lime or ½ lemon

2 tablespoons olive or vegetable oil

3 tablespoons Seafood Adobo (see page 16) or other favorite dry rub

1. Sprinkle the fish with the lime juice and then let sit for 3 to 5 minutes; pat dry with a paper towel.

2. Brush the oil over the surface of the fish evenly.

3. Season the fish with the dry rub.

4. Place on a rack in a preheated to medium (275 to 300 degrees) smoker and smoke for 25 to 35 minutes until the fish reaches an internal temperature of 130 to 140 degrees.

NOTE: A piece of foil loosely placed over the fish (shiny side towards the fish) will help keep it moist.

ORANGE-FLAVORED SMOKED TuRKEy LeGs

TURKEY WAS NATIVE to the New World and remains the poultry of choice in the Yucatan peninsula of Mexico today. The bright orange tang and the rich earthy achiote bring out the best in this humble bird. By smoking the turkey, you will capture the flavors of the "Pibil" or pit, an important method in Mayan cooking. Turkey legs could be served whole along with Tropical Fruit Salsa (see page 72) or Charred Cherry Tomato Salsa (see page 78), or the meat may be shredded for tacos, enchiladas, Mexican tortas (sandwiches), tostadas or quesadillas. This recipe will also produce an excellent whole smoked turkey. Increase the marinade and the cooking times according to the total weight of the bird.

SERVES 6 AS A MAIN COURSE

6 turkey legs or leg and thigh quarters (4 to 6 pounds)

1 to 1½ times the recipe for Orange-Achiote Marinade (see page 21)

1. Rinse the turkey legs and pat dry with a paper towel.

2. In a nonreactive bowl or a large plastic bag, place the turkey and the marinade and mix well to coat; seal tightly and refrigerate. Marinate for at least 2 hours and preferably overnight.

3. Remove the turkey from the refrigerator 30 to 45 minutes prior to smoking.

4. Reserve a cup of the marinade for basting.

5. Place the legs on a rack in a smoker preheated to medium high (275 to 300 degrees).

6. Smoke for about 1½ to 2 hours, turning the legs every 20 to 30 minutes and brushing with a little of the marinade to maintain moisture. The turkey is done when the meat next to the bone is at least 165 degrees.

NOTE: *Do not baste with the marinade during the last 20 to 30 minutes of cooking. Discard the unused marinade.*

*Orange-Flavored
Smoked Turkey Legs*

SMOKED WHOLE ChickeN
WITH GARLIC, HERB & CUMIN MARINADE

SMOKING A CHICKEN is a more interesting alternative to roasting and the results can be used in many ways: as a main course, for sandwiches or tacos, and in pasta dishes and salads. With a simple marinade like the one in this recipe, the task is easy and does not require a lot of attention during the cooking process. Any of the marinades or dry rubs in the first chapter will also work to season the chicken.

SERVES 4 TO 6 (DEPENDING ON THE SIZE OF THE CHICKEN)

1 fryer or roaster chicken, 3½ to 5½ pounds

Garlic, Herb and Cumin Marinade (see page 23)

1. Rinse the chicken and pat dry with paper towels.

2. In a nonreactive bowl or a large plastic bag, place the chicken and the marinade and mix well to coat; seal tightly and refrigerate for 1 to 3 hours.

3. Place in a smoker preheated to medium-high (275 to 300 degrees) and smoke for 1¾ to 2½ hours until the internal temperature of the thigh meat is 165 to 170 degrees.

4. Let chicken rest for 10 to 15 minutes before cutting.

Smoked Whole Chicken
with Garlic, Herb and
Cumin Marinade

Smoked Vegetables

When vegetables are smoked, they take on a completely different character. Smoking also helps to preserve the vegetables, providing an excellent solution to an overabundant summer garden. After they are smoked, many vegetables could also be frozen for several months. Smoked vegetables may be used as a side dish, to fill quesadillas, as an addition to salads and pasta dishes, or made into interesting salsas. A stovetop smoker is excellent for this type of smoking.

Sliced or diced squash or eggplant, halved or quartered tomatoes, corn on the cob, seeded and stemmed sweet peppers and chiles, mushrooms, whole green beans, small peeled onions, peeled garlic, and so on.

Enough olive or vegetable oil to lightly coat the vegetables

Your favorite dry rub (see pages 14–20) OR salt and pepper to season

NOTE: The smaller the vegetables are cut, the faster they will cook and the more smoke flavor will be infused, size according to your needs. You may also cut smaller pieces after they have been smoked.

1. Toss the vegetables with the oil to coat.

2. Season with the rub or salt and pepper.

3. Place on a rack or piece of foil in a preheated smoker on medium heat (275 to 300 degrees).

4. Smoke until the vegetables reach their desired doneness (for bite-sized diced zucchini or other summer squash it takes about 20 to 25 minutes).

Vegetables ready to smoke

Salsas & Sauces

Salsas are a simple yet impressive way to complement many grilled foods. They pack a lot of flavor and lend an acidic, spicy and sometimes sweet contrast to grilled meats and seafood. Salsas are low-fat and healthy and may be counted as a serving or two of vegetables or fruit. They also provide convenience since they are easy to prepare and can usually be made in advance. The simple combination of a grilled piece of meat or fish topped with a salsa and served with a side dish and/or a salad makes an interesting, quick and complete meal. There are many approaches to salsas: some are simple, fairly liquid, condiments intended merely to add a little extra spice and acidity; others are complex concoctions that require a number of ingredients and the application of sophisticated preparation techniques; and there are also some chunky contemporary creations that practically transcend the definition of a salsa and function as salads or side dishes.

While chile heat is generally an important component of a salsa, and I am a big fan of piquancy, I feel that the heat is only one part of the equation. The balance of sweet and sour, saltiness and aroma is crucial to a good salsa. If you are going to use incendiary levels of chile heat, make sure that the supporting flavors match the intensity of that spiciness. If all that can be tasted is the heat, I believe that the salsa is a failure. A great salsa should stimulate the taste buds, not numb them. The following are a few salsas that I often use to accompany grilled foods. Feel free to use your imagination to create variations to develop your own original salsa flavors.

Black Bean and Fire-Roasted Chile Salsa (see page 76),
Tropical Fruit Salsa (page 74), and Charred Cherry or
Pear Tomato Salsa (page 77)

TROPICAL Fruit sALsa

THE SWEETNESS OF FRUIT is often a perfect complement to savory grilled meats and fish. This procedure gives you a lot of flexibility in your choices of fruits and is really several recipes under one title. You could use only one type of fruit like mango or papaya; or make a version using only melon; or you could combine two, three, or several fruits. The choices will often depend on what you are pairing it with, the season, or what is available. Fruit salsa is often more of a side dish that is paired with the main course instead of only a flavoring.

Makes 2½ cups

1 small to medium red or white onion, peeled and diced

2 cups fresh, ripe fruits (mango, pineapple, papaya, melons, oranges, kiwi, etc.), peeled, seeded (as appropriate) and diced into ¼- to ⅜-inch cubes

½ red bell pepper, seeded and inner membranes removed, diced small

1 or 2 jalapeño or serrano chiles, stemmed, seeded and finely chopped

2 tablespoons fresh lime juice

1 tablespoon orange juice (optional)

¼ cup chopped mint and/or cilantro

Dash of salt

1 teaspoon vegetable oil (optional to help preserve the freshness and add some shine)

Honey or sugar for additional sweetness, if needed

1. Place the onion in a strainer and rinse with hot tap water for about 20 seconds, then rinse with cold water until cooled to room temperature (this helps to eliminate the gassy flavor of raw onions).

2. Combine all of the ingredients, mix well and taste. Add more sweetener if needed.

NOTE: *Store the salsa in the refrigerator but take it out 20 to 30 minutes prior to serving to enhance the flavor.*

GRILLED PINEAPPLE SALSA

WHILE IT MAY SEEM UNUSUAL to treat pineapple this way, grilling brings out the natural sugars, develops additional complexity of flavors and the smoky taste is an excellent complement to spicy, rich and savory foods. It is particularly useful when you encounter a pineapple that is a little under ripe and lacks sweetness.

MAKES ABOUT 2½ CUPS

1 medium-sized fresh, ripe pineapple, skinned, cored and cut into ¼-inch-thick slices

2 tablespoons granulated sugar (you may want to use a little more if the pineapple is a bit sour)

2 teaspoons ground allspice (optional)

1 teaspoon salt, divided

½ red onion, peeled and sliced into ¼-inch-thick rounds

Vegetable oil spray

½ red bell pepper, seeded and the inner membranes removed

2 serrano, 2 jalapeño or 1 to 2 habanero chiles (each chile gives a little different flavor but they will all taste good)

2 tablespoons fresh lime juice

1 tablespoon apple cider or rice vinegar

¼ cup chopped cilantro or mint (or a combination of the two; fresh oregano or sage is also interesting with pineapple)

1 tablespoon vegetable oil (optional)

1. Preheat your grill to medium.

2. Evenly sprinkle the pineapple slices with the sugar, allspice and ½ of the salt.

3. Lightly coat the pineapple and the onion slices with the vegetable spray.

4. Char grill the pineapple, onion, red pepper, and chiles until the pineapple and onion slices have developed grill marks and are a little charred. The chiles should be well-charred.

5. Stem and seed the chiles and mince.

6. Dice the pineapple, red pepper and onion slices in ¼-inch cubes.

7. Combine the grilled items with the lime juice, vinegar, remaining salt, and cilantro and/or mint. Mix well and add the optional oil if you want to add a little richness and shine to the salsa.

NOTE: If the salsa is still a little sour, you may add a little honey or sugar to balance the flavors.

BLACK BEAN & FIRE-ROASTED ChiLE sALsA

THIS SALSA COULD ALSO DOUBLE as a cold side dish if served in larger quantities. It adds a Southwestern flair to any grilled meal. Other colors of beans could be substituted for the black beans. Sometimes the normally mild to medium-hot poblano chiles can be either very hot or not piquant at all. Taste them before you put them in the recipe. It is easier to add chiles than subtract them. If it is not hot enough, you might try adding some of your favorite bottled hot sauce, chipotle chiles in adobo or finely minced jalapeño.

MAKES ABOUT 4½ CUPS

2¾ cups cooked black beans, well rinsed

⅓ cup diced red or white onions, rinsed

1 clove garlic, crushed and finely minced

3 to 4 poblano chiles, roasted, peeled, seeded, and diced
    (Anaheim or New Mexican green could also be used)

½ teaspoon toasted, ground cumin seed

¾ cup diced tomatoes

⅛ cup sherry vinegar or apple cider vinegar

1 tablespoon fresh lime juice

2 teaspoons salt

Black pepper to taste

2 tablespoons extra virgin olive oil

2 tablespoons chopped fresh marjoram or cilantro leaves OR
    1 tablespoon toasted Mexican oregano

1. Toss all of the ingredients together, allow the flavors to develop for about 10 minutes and then taste and adjust the seasonings.

2. Serve at or near room temperature; refrigerate to store. Will store for 4 to 5 days.

CHARRED CHERRY OR PEAR TOMATO SALSA

THIS IS A VERSATILE SALSA that also keeps well. The use of small tomatoes in various colors dresses it up but you could also make it by using larger tomatoes and then coarsely chopping them. In Mexico, many salsas make use of roasted or charred tomatoes for their extra depth of flavor and this is a contemporary take on that tradition. You could use this as a traditional salsa for tacos and dips or as an accompaniment to many grilled meats.

MAKES ABOUT 3 CUPS

Salt to taste

1 medium white or red onion, peeled and sliced
   in ½-inch rounds

3 cups (about 1¼ pounds) cherry or pear tomatoes
   (red, yellow, orange or a mix)

1 teaspoon + 1 tablespoon extra virgin olive oil

2 cloves roasted garlic, peeled and thinly sliced

2 teaspoons to 2 tablespoons chopped chipotle chiles in
   adobo (depending on your heat tolerance)

1 tablespoon chopped fresh marjoram, oregano or cilantro
   leaves (2 teaspoons toasted, dried Mexican oregano
   could also be used)

1½ tablespoons sherry vinegar or apple cider vinegar or lime
   juice

Salt and pepper to taste

Sugar as needed

Wood chunks or chips for smoke flavor

1. Preheat your grill to medium-high.

2. Salt the onion slices and grill until browned and a little charred around the edges. Remove from the heat and cool. Chop into ½-inch pieces.

3. Toss the tomatoes in 1 teaspoon oil and char on the grill, using wood chips for flavor, turning occasionally until they have some black spots and are beginning to give off a little juice, yet remain firm. Remove from the heat and place in a bowl to capture all of the liquid.

4. Combine the onion, tomatoes, garlic, chiles, herbs, vinegar, and remaining oil and let sit for 10 to 15 minutes for the flavors to develop.

5. Taste and season with salt and pepper and, if needed, add a little sugar to balance the acidity.

Salsa Fresca

THIS UBIQUITOUS, BASIC SALSA is often called *Salsa Mexicana* both because it is a typical salsa throughout the country and because it has the red, green and white colors of the Mexican flag. In the Yucatan and in Quintana Roo, where it is made with chile habanero instead of jalapeño, it is called *Xni-Pec* (shnee-peck), which is the Maya word for a wet dog's nose; one of the side effects you may experience with that fiery version of this salsa.

MAKES ABOUT 3 CUPS

4 to 5 ripe plum tomatoes, diced ¼ inch thick

¼ teaspoon finely minced garlic (optional)

½ cup finely chopped red or white onion, rinsed briefly in hot and then cold water

2 tablespoons fresh lime juice OR mild vinegar such as apple cider vinegar, rice wine vinegar or a mix of both

2 or 3 fresh jalapeño or serrano chiles, seeded (if jalapeño) and finely chopped

Salt to taste

¼ cup coarsely chopped cilantro

1 tablespoon olive oil (optional)

1. Put the tomatoes, garlic, onion, lime juice or vinegar, chiles, and salt in a bowl and mix well. You may coarsely puree this mixture in a food processor or you can leave the ingredients intact for more texture. Taste after 10 minutes, adjust the chile and lime juice to suit your taste. Add the cilantro. (The cilantro is reserved until after the adjustment so that it does not mask the flavors of the chile and the lime. It takes about 10 minutes for the interaction of the lime's acidity and the chile heat to stabilize.)

2. Add the oil, if desired. It will make the salsa shiny, add a bit of flavor and help to preserve it. Let the mixture sit for 30 minutes to allow the flavors to develop. The ideal serving temperature is 55 to 60 degrees, so don't serve it directly from the refrigerator.

GREEN CHILE ChutNeY

OUTSTANDING WITH GRILLED SEAFOOD, this salsa is versatile enough to use with many things. I use it to flavor mayonnaise, garnish soup, as a canapé topping, or in quesadillas. The sweet and sour combination and long cooking time tempers the heat of the chiles, although you still cannot miss them. There is nothing like the flavor of New Mexican green chiles; however, poblano or Anaheim chiles could be used instead.

MAKES ABOUT 2 CUPS

24 New Mexican green chiles (about 2 pounds), roasted, peeled, seeded and diced about ⅜-inch square

1 red bell pepper, roasted, peeled, seeded and diced about ⅜-inch square

2 tablespoons diced onion

2 cloves garlic, peeled

⅛ teaspoon ground coriander (optional)

3 bay leaves, toasted

⅔ cup brown sugar

¼ cup apple cider vinegar

1 cup water

½ teaspoon salt

NOTE: 3 cups (24 ounces) of frozen (thawed for use), roasted and diced green chiles may be substituted.

1. In a heavy saucepan or skillet, heat all of the ingredients to boiling. Continue boiling for 10 to 15 minutes, stirring occasionally, until the mixture begins to thicken.

2. Reduce the heat and stir more frequently, as needed to prevent burning as the mixture continues to thicken. When most, but not all, of the liquid has evaporated, remove from the heat and take out the bay leaves.

3. Cool a bit and then taste and add salt as needed.

4. Serve warm or cool.

NOTE: This chutney may be kept in the refrigerator for several weeks.

Salsa Verde

GREEN TAQUERIA-STYLE SAUCE

This is a typical version of a typical salsa. As the name implies, great on tacos, but also with grilled meats, with chips as a dip, and along with empanadas or quesadillas. Variations could include boiling the ingredients or a making a raw Salsa Verde like the Salsa Mexicana, either chunky, pureed or liquefied (reduce the garlic to 1 clove minced and dice the onion in the raw variation). The lemony flavor of the tomatillos is a good contrast to rich or fatty foods.

MAKES ABOUT 2 CUPS

1 dozen tomatillos, husked and rinsed

6 cloves garlic, peeled

3 to 4 serrano chiles, stems removed (or jalapeño chiles with seeds removed for a little milder salsa)

1 small white onion, sliced in 3 rounds

1 bunch fresh cilantro

Juice of ½ lime (about 1 tablespoon)

½ teaspoon sugar (if needed to balance the acidity)

Salt to taste

1. Lightly char the tomatillos on a grill, on a comal or in a heavy skillet along with the garlic, chiles and onion for about 5 to 6 minutes, or until they are somewhat browned, charred and caramelized. The tomatillos should still retain some of their bright green color. Cool.

2. Coarsely chop the cilantro leaves. Separately chop the garlic, onions and chiles.

3. Place tomatillos and roasted onions, garlic and chiles in a blender or food processor and blend, adding a little water if necessary. The sauce should be thick. Pour the sauce into a bowl. Add cilantro, lime juice, sugar (if the salsa is too tart), and season with salt to taste.

GAZPACHO VEGETABLE SalsA

THIS SALSA TAKES ITS CUE from the classic flavors of gazpacho, a cold soup from Spain that has many variations throughout Latin America, with a little chile and cilantro to add some zing. It goes well with most grilled foods, especially seafood. It could also serve as a side dish as part of a grilled menu.

MAKES ABOUT 2½ CUPS

1 medium cucumber, peeled and seeded

1 or 2 poblano chiles, stemmed, seeded and inner membrane ribs removed (1 sweet red pepper may be used in place of or along with the chile for a milder salsa)

1 medium red onion, peeled

3 plum or 1 to 2 larger, ripe tomatoes

¼ cup Spanish sherry vinegar or red wine vinegar

¼ cup chopped cilantro (optional, you could also use flat-leaf parsley)

Juice of ½ lime (about 1 tablespoon)

Salt and pepper to taste

3 tablespoons extra virgin olive oil

1. Dice all of the vegetables in ¼-inch cubes.

2. Rinse the onion in hot tap water for 20 seconds and then 20 seconds more in cold water to cool (this will remove the gassy flavor from the onions).

3. Mix the diced vegetables with the vinegar, cilantro and lime juice and season to taste with salt and pepper.

4. Stir in the oil.

5. Serve at or near room temperature.

CILANTRO-PUMPKINSEED Pesto

A TWIST ON CLASSIC BASIL PESTO, this sauce calls for cilantro for the herb and pumpkinseed in place of pine nuts and is based on the Mexican Pipián sauce. I use it for grilled seafood, chicken or pork and it could be used as a pasta sauce or a dressing for potato salad too. You may adjust the chile heat by substituting hotter or milder chiles, as you prefer. See a photo of the pesto on page 49.

MAKES ABOUT 1⅔ CUPS

1 or 2 poblano, New Mexican green or jalapeño chiles, fire-roasted, peeled and seeded

6 to 8 cloves garlic, roasted and peeled

1 cup green pumpkinseeds, pan roasted until most of the seeds have popped and the edges are slightly browned, then cooled

1 bunch cilantro, well washed and the last 2 inches of the root end cut off and discarded

1½ teaspoons salt

Juice of ½ lime (1 tablespoon)

2 to 3 tablespoons cool water or more as needed to make a smooth puree

¼ cup extra virgin olive oil

1. Puree all ingredients, except the oil, in a food processor or blender until smooth (with a blender a little more water is needed).

2. Taste for salt and chile heat and adjust as needed.

3. Blend in the oil.

4. Serve at room temperature.

NOTE: *May be stored in the refrigerator up to 3 days with plastic wrap on the surface to prevent browning.*

Piñon-Apple Chutney

THIS IS A DELICIOUS COOKED, mild salsa highlighting the flavors of autumn in New Mexico. I originally created this chutney to accompany Red Chile–Apple Cider Glazed Pork Chops (see page 38), and it also goes well with many other different grilled or smoked meats. Piñon-Apple Chutney will keep for several weeks in your refrigerator and also adapts well to home canning.

MAKES 2¾ CUPS (8 TO 10 SERVINGS)

½ cup diced onions

1 clove garlic, sliced

1 cup apple cider

⅓ cup apple cider vinegar

¾ cup water

¼ cup honey

Pinch of salt

2 tablespoons New Mexican red chile powder, mild or medium-hot, lightly toasted

½ teaspoon ground allspice

1 teaspoon ground canela (Mexican cinnamon)

2 cups fresh peeled or frozen apples diced in ½-inch dice (½ cup reserved)

½ cup toasted pine nuts

Juice of ½ lime or lemon

¼ cup raisins or dried currants

1. Place all ingredients except pine nuts, reserved apples, lime juice and raisins in a heavy saucepan and bring to a low boil. Allow liquid to reduce by half and then add raisins and reserved apples.

2. Reduce heat to simmer and continue cooking until most of the liquid has evaporated.

3. Stir in pine nuts, cool 5 minutes, add lime juice and adjust seasonings.

4. Serve warm or at room temperature.

SMOKED CHIPTOLE CHILE–HERB Butter

MELTING A FLAVORED BUTTER on something that is hot off the grill is an easy way to make a simple preparation interesting and tasty. This one, with the smoky heat of the chipotle and the fresh herb, citrus and roasted garlic aroma, is one of my favorites for grilled items. You could use it for meats, poultry, seafood or vegetables. When you make the butter, if you make enough extra, you can save it in the freezer. Simply form the butter into a log shape and wrap it several times in plastic wrap. When you need some, just soften it and carefully slice off portions to use and rewrap the rest. Allow the butter to soften well before putting it on anything before serving. A portion for an average piece of grilled steak would be about a tablespoon.

MAKES ABOUT 1¼ CUP

2 sticks (1 cup) sweet cream butter, softened to
    room temperature

4 chipotle chiles in adobo, finely minced

1 teaspoon finely minced lime zest

1 teaspoon finely minced orange zest (optional)

10 to 12 medium cloves garlic

2 tablespoons minced fresh chives or 1 scallion, trimmed
    and finely minced

1 tablespoon chopped fresh marjoram, cilantro or
    epazote leaves

1½ teaspoons salt

1. In a stand mixer fitted with a paddle or by hand in a bowl with a heavy wooden spoon, mix all of the ingredients to combine well.

2. Taste and reserve what you will use immediately. Store the remainder as described above.

SMOKED TOMATO VINAIGRETTE

THIS DRESSING BECOMES incredibly flavorful with the addition of the smoked tomatoes and garlic. Originally intended as a salad dressing, it can be used as a delectable sauce for grilled meats, poultry and seafood.

½ pound smoked tomatoes (see page 70)

6 cloves smoked garlic (see page 70)

¼ teaspoon + ½ teaspoon coarse salt

2 scallions (or Grilled Scallion Garnish, see page 96), thinly sliced

1 teaspoon chopped fresh marjoram or oregano leaves
    OR 1 tablespoon chopped flat-leaf parsley or cilantro leaves

½ teaspoon coarsely ground black pepper

¼ cup Spanish sherry, balsamic or red wine vinegar

½ cup olive oil

1. Puree in a blender or hand chop the tomatoes, depending on the texture desired.

2. Finely hand chop the garlic with ¼ teaspoon salt.

3. Mix the tomatoes, garlic, scallions, herbs, remaining salt, pepper, and vinegar in a bowl.

4. Whisk in the oil a little at a time.

5. Store refrigerated, up to 5 to 7 days, in a tightly sealed glass or stainless steel container and warm a little at room temperature before serving.

Chimichurri

THIS ARGENTINEAN GREEN HERB SALSA is usually used as an accompaniment to grilled beef but is also good as a marinade or brush-on seasoning for fish, shrimp or poultry. For a southwestern flavor, use cilantro instead of parsley. See a photo on page 35.

MAKES ABOUT 1½ CUPS

8 cloves garlic, peeled and minced

2 jalapeño chiles, stemmed, seeded and finely chopped

¾ cup parsley leaves (flat-leaf variety)

2 tablespoons fresh oregano leaves

3 tablespoons Spanish sherry vinegar or red wine vinegar

½ teaspoon toasted cumin seed (optional)

1 teaspoon freshly ground black pepper

1½ teaspoons salt

½ cup extra virgin olive oil

1. Blend all ingredients in a food processor until smooth.

2. Serve at or near room temperature but store in the refrigerator up to 3 days.

SALADS

THE COOLNESS AND FRESHNESS of a salad makes for a great complement to spicy, grilled main courses. Prepare salads in advance to be all set to serve when the grill items are ready.

JICAMA FIESTA SLAW

JICAMA IS A ROOT VEGETABLE in the legume or bean family. It is used extensively in Latin American–Mexican cooking. Jicama has the texture of a fresh water chestnut and a slightly sweet, bright flavor that combines well with sweet, savory and spicy-hot flavors. This salad may be prepared up to one day in advance of serving.

SERVES 4 TO 6

1 medium-sized jicama (about 1 pound), peeled

2 to 3 carrots (about ¾ cup), peeled

1 medium red onion, peeled and sliced very thin (julienne), cut into 1¼-inch-long pieces, then rinsed briefly in hot then cold water (to remove the gassy taste)

1 red or yellow bell pepper, stemmed, seeded, inner membrane removed and sliced very thin (julienne), then cut into 1¼-inch-long pieces

1 or 2 jalapeño chiles, stemmed, seeded, and cut in half lengthwise, then sliced very thin across

Juice of ½ orange (⅛ cup)

1 tablespoon lime juice

1 teaspoon finely minced lime zest

½ teaspoon salt

¼ cup chopped mint and/or cilantro leaves

1½ tablespoons olive oil

1. On a mandoline set to fine julienne, the coarse side of a box-type grater or the grater attachment to a food processor, shred the jicama and carrots.

2. Toss together all of the ingredients, except the oil, and mix well. Taste and adjust seasonings if needed.

3. Add the oil and toss again.

4. Serve immediately or store, tightly covered, in the refrigerator (remove from the refrigerator 20 to 30 minutes before serving).

Jicama Fiesta Slaw

Spicy Yam Salad

THE EARTHY-SWEET FLAVOR and orange color of the yams combine with the rich smokiness of the chipotle chiles in a not-so-traditional take on potato salad. This dish may be made ahead of time and transports well to picnics and on camping excursions. Feel free to substitute sweet potatoes for the yams. An even more colorful variation uses half purple potatoes and half yams; cook the potatoes and yams separately as they may cook at different rates.

SERVES 4 TO 6

1 teaspoon honey

1 teaspoon mild vinegar

1 tablespoon lime juice

1 to 2 tablespoons chipotle chiles in adobo, pureed or finely chopped

½ teaspoon minced garlic

Pinch of ground cloves

1 teaspoon + 1½ teaspoons salt

1 tablespoon olive oil

2½ pounds yams or sweet potatoes, peeled and diced into bite-sized chunks

⅓ cup mayonnaise

1 tablespoon prepared yellow mustard

½ cup red onion, diced and rinsed

1 teaspoon ground black pepper

¼ cup chopped cilantro or flat-leaf parsley

3 hard-boiled eggs, peeled and coarsely chopped

1. Dissolve the honey in the vinegar and lime juice; add the chiles, garlic cloves, 1 teaspoon salt and oil. Mix well.

2. Cook the yams in 2 quarts boiling water seasoned with 1½ teaspoons salt until cooked through and tender, yet still firm, about 8 to 10 minutes. Drain and toss with the chile mixture, then spread out to cool rapidly.

3. When the yams have cooled, mix them well with the mayonnaise, mustard, onion, pepper and cilantro. Gently fold in the hard-boiled eggs.

4. Refrigerate at least 30 minutes prior to serving.

Spicy Yam Salad

GRILLED YELLOW POTATO &
RoaSTED PePpeR SaLaD

POTATOES ORIGINATED IN PERU and have been cultivated in many colors and shapes; a true New World ingredient. The yellow potatoes were first raised in Finland and now they have become popular everywhere. There are a number of domestic varieties available. The waxy texture and the buttery flavor make them perfect for grilling. The resulting potato salad lends a new meaning to "steak and potatoes."

SERVES 4 TO 6

2 ½ to 3 pounds medium-sized yellow potatoes, well scrubbed and cut into ⅜-inch-thick slices

1 tablespoon + 1½ teaspoons salt

2 tablespoons olive oil mixed with 1 teaspoon chopped garlic (about 2 cloves)

2 to 3 teaspoons dry rub, your favorite or what you have on hand (see pages 14–20)

2 tablespoons apple cider, Spanish sherry or wine vinegar

1 tablespoon Dijon or other premium mustard

½ teaspoon Worcestershire sauce

2 scallions, trimmed and thinly sliced

½ teaspoon black pepper

2 red peppers and 1 poblano chile, roasted, peeled, seeded and cut into 1-inch triangles

¼ cup olive oil

¼ cup chopped flat-leaf parsley OR 1 tablespoon fresh marjoram, thyme, oregano or a combination

1. Blanch the potato slices in 2 ½ quarts boiling water with 1 tablespoon salt added until just beginning to soften (about 5 to 6 minutes). The potatoes must remain firm. Cool rapidly, and then pat dry with a paper towel.

2. Brush the potatoes with the oil-garlic mixture, then season with the dry rub. Let sit for 15 to 20 minutes.

3. Cook on the char grill over medium heat until well browned with nice grill marks. Turn and cook the other side the same.

4. Remove from the grill and cool.

5. In a bowl, mix the vinegar, mustard, Worcestershire sauce, scallions, remaining salt and black pepper. Stir in the roasted peppers and the potatoes. Add the oil and parsley and carefully toss.

6. Serve at room temperature.

Grilled Yellow Potato and
Roasted Pepper Salad

Red Chile Caesar Salad
with Grilled Garlic Croutons

THERE IS A LOT OF FOLKLORE associated with the origin of Caesar salad. Regardless of the origin, this has become an American classic. I have added a slight southwestern twist to the dressing and included an option of char grilling the croutons. I prefer leaving the lettuce leaves whole, but you may chop or tear them into bite-sized pieces if you prefer.

MAKES 4 TO 6 SALADS

1 large head romaine lettuce, outer leaves discarded, stems trimmed, leaves separated, washed and dried

Red Chile Caesar Salad Dressing (see page 94)

⅓ to ½ cup grated fresh Parmesan, Romano or Mexican Cotija cheese

Garlic Croutons (recipe below)

Freshly ground black pepper to taste

4 to 6 anchovy fillets, whole or chopped, for garnish (optional)

1. Place the lettuce in a mixing or salad bowl.

2. Drizzle with ½ to ⅔ cup of the dressing.

3. Sprinkle in half of the cheese and toss until the lettuce is well coated.

4. Plate the salad and garnish with Garlic Croutons, remaining cheese, freshly ground black pepper and the optional anchovies.

Garlic Infused Olive-Canola Oil

¾ cup extra virgin olive oil

½ cup canola or other vegetable oil

10 cloves garlic, peeled

1. Blend olive oil with canola or other vegetable oil.

2. Add garlic and puree in a blender for 15 seconds.

3. Let sit 15 minutes and then strain. Discard garlic.

Garlic Croutons

¼ teaspoon salt

¼ cup Garlic Infused Olive-Canola Oil

12 slices baguette or other small-diameter, crusty bread, sliced ¼ inch thick OR 2 cups cubed bread

1. Mix the salt with the oil.

2. Brush the bread slices on both sides with the oil (if using cubed bread, slowly drizzle the oil over the cubes while gently tossing until evenly coated).

3. Let sit for a few minutes to allow the oil to absorb.

4. Grill over medium heat until grill marks develop and edges are lightly browned and the bread is crispy.

NOTE: You can also bake the cubes on a baking sheet in a 325-degree oven, stirring occasionally, until golden brown and crispy (about 15 to 20 minutes).

Red Chile Caesar Salad with
Grilled Garlic Croutons

Red Chile Caesar Salad Dressing

Makes 2 cups

3 egg yolks, room temperature or coddled for 1 minute

1 tablespoon Dijon or other full-flavored mustard

2 tablespoons lime juice

2 anchovy fillets or 1 tablespoon anchovy puree

¼ cup cold water

¼ cup Spanish sherry vinegar or white wine vinegar

2 teaspoons Worcestershire sauce

1 to 2 tablespoons New Mexican red chile powder, lightly toasted OR chipotle chile in adobo puree

¼ teaspoon salt

1 teaspoon ground black pepper

1 cup Garlic Infused Olive-Canola Oil

1. Mix all ingredients, except oil, in food processor for 15 seconds.

2. With machine running slowly, add oil until a smooth creamy consistency is achieved.

Avocado Grapefruit Salad

An unusual, yet satisfying combination that lends a summery feel to menus year round, this salad is an ideal companion to rich and/or spicy foods. Pink or red grapefruit has a striking color to contrast the avocado, but white grapefruit may also be used. The grapefruit may be sectioned ahead of time but the avocado should not be sliced until just before serving.

Serves 4 to 6

Watercress, arugula, or lettuce

2 to 3 pink or ruby-red grapefruits, peeled and sectioned with a sharp knife to remove the membrane (reserve juice)

2 large or 3 to 4 small ripe avocados, peeled and sliced ⅛ inch thick

1 to 2 serrano or jalapeño chiles, stemmed, seeded, cut in half lengthwise, then sliced very thin

½ teaspoon salt

2 tablespoons chopped cilantro

2 tablespoons lime juice

1 teaspoon sugar

2 teaspoons olive or vegetable oil

1. Line the serving dish with the greens.

2. Arrange the grapefruit slices around the dish in a spiral, alternating with the avocado slices.

3. Scatter the chile strips evenly over the fruit, sprinkle with salt.

4. Evenly scatter the cilantro.

5. Mix the grapefruit and lime juices with the sugar and oil and drizzle over the entire salad.

6. Serve cool but not overly chilled.

Sonoran Grilled Steak sAlad

THE STATE OF SONORA IN MEXICO is comprised mostly of desert; however, irrigation has made possible vegetable and citrus farming along with cattle ranching. This salad uses all three of those components to create a main dish salad that is perfect for a lunch or light supper. The dressing works well for other salads or as a marinade for grilled poultry or seafood.

SERVES 4 TO 6

2 to 3 pounds sirloin, flank or strip loin steak

2 to 3 tablespoons Mexican Adobo (see page 17) or Smoky Chipotle (see page 15)

12 to 16 ounces mixed lettuces (romaine, iceberg, red leaf, butter, etc.)

1 medium cucumber, peeled and sliced

2 to 3 ripe tomatoes, sliced

1 medium red onion, peeled and thinly sliced

3 to 4 Anaheim or 2 to 3 poblano chiles, roasted, peeled, stemmed, seeded and cut into ½-inch-wide strips

2 medium avocados, sliced

Orange-Anise Dressing (recipe below)

6 corn tortillas, cut in ½-inch strips and fried crispy (packaged corn tortilla chips may be used)

3 ounces crumbled Cotija or feta cheese (optional)

1. Rub steaks with the dry rub. Grill the steak medium-rare to medium on a hot grill. Rest steak for 10 minutes then slice thin.

2. On a large platter or serving dish, arrange the lettuce topped with the cucumber, tomatoes, onion and chiles. Place the avocado slices around the edges and fan the sliced steak across the top.

3. Drizzle with the dressing and garnish with the crispy tortilla strips and the cheese.

Orange-Anise Dressing

½ cup freshly squeezed orange juice

1 teaspoon finely minced orange zest

1 tablespoon lime juice

2 teaspoons mild vinegar

1 clove garlic, minced

2 tablespoons chopped cilantro

1 tablespoon anise seeds, lightly toasted and ground (you can substitute 1 tablespoon Pernod liqueur here)

½ cup olive oil

¼ cup vegetable oil

½ teaspoon salt

½ teaspoon ground black pepper

1. Combine all ingredients and whisk well to blend.

SIDES/ACCOMPANIMENTS

A WONDERFUL FOCAL POINT in a menu calls for a brilliant supporting cast in the form of accompaniments and side dishes. The following recipes are for dishes designed to complement the main courses in this book. Some are cooked on the grill and others just taste good with grilled food.

GRILLED SCALLION GARNISH

SCALLIONS CHARRED BRIEFLY over fire are an excellent embellishment to complete a grilled menu. It takes just minutes to accomplish and adds an elegant final touch. If you can find onions that are a little larger with a small bulb as you would see in Mexico, even better; however, the smaller varieties that are more common are fine.

ENOUGH TO GARNISH 6 MAIN COURSES

1 or 2 bunches scallions (2 per person if they are small, 1 if larger onions are used), washed and trimmed

1 tablespoon olive or vegetable oil

1 to 2 teaspoons of your favorite dry rub (see pages 14–20) OR salt and pepper to taste

1. Brush the onions with the oil to evenly coat.

2. Sprinkle with the dry rub or salt and pepper.

3. Grill over flames or hot coals until marks develop and scallions have softened a little.

4. Turn over and continue cooking so that the second side matches the first.

5. Place on top of or to the side of grilled entrees as a garnish.

Grilled Scallion Garnish

GRILLED CaLaBaCiTaS

CALABACITAS, LITERALLY MEANING *"LITTLE SQUASHES"* in Spanish, are prepared throughout Latin America and the American Southwest. There are probably as many recipes for this dish as there are cooks making it. More commonly, the squash and other ingredients are sautéed and often cream, sour cream or cheese is added. Chiles and corn are also included in calabacitas. You could add a little Fire-Roasted Corn (see page 103), grilled mushrooms or tomato wedges if you like. Cooking the squash over fire or coals, creates a more sophisticated and lower-fat version that presents well.

SERVES 4 TO 6

1 tablespoon minced garlic (about 4 to 5 cloves)

3 to 4 tablespoons olive or vegetable oil

1 to 2 red or yellow sweet bell peppers

2 poblano chiles or 3 to 4 New Mexican green or Anaheim chiles

2 pounds small to medium squash (zucchini, yellow summer or crookneck, Mexican green, etc.)

1 medium white or red onion, peeled and cut into 3 or 4 round slices ³⁄₈ inch thick

1 to 2 tablespoons Mexican Adobo (see page 17), Mojo (see page 18) or other dry rub OR salt and pepper to taste

Juice of 2 limes (about ¹⁄₄ cup)

1 tablespoon total: chopped fresh marjoram, oregano and/or thyme OR lightly toasted, dried Mexican oregano or dried thyme

1. Combine the garlic and oil and set aside to infuse.

2. Remove the stem, seeds and inner membranes from each sweet pepper and chile and cut off both ends so that you have uniform pieces that will cook evenly on the grill.

3. Slice the squash lengthwise in ³⁄₈-inch-thick pieces. *NOTE: First make two very thin slices on opposing sides of each squash to remove the skin and help make the slices for cooking more uniform.*

4. Brush the squash, onion slices, chiles, and sweet peppers on both sides with the garlic oil.

5. Sprinkle the dry rub evenly over all of the vegetables.

6. Grill over a moderate flame or coals until well-defined marks develop, rotate each piece 90 degrees to create cross marks. *NOTE: Start the peppers and chiles skin side down.*

7. Turn over each piece and grill until cooked through but still a little firm.

8. Remove from heat and arrange on a platter.

9. Sprinkle the lime juice and herbs over all and serve (you may want to re-warm the calabacitas in the broiler or oven just before serving).

NOTE: Cut vegetables into bite-sized or manageable pieces if you prefer.

Grilled Calabacitas

Rice & Beans

THIS RECIPE COMES FROM the Maya-inhabited areas of the Yucatan and Quintana Roo in Mexico and in Guatemala. The name is usually listed in English even on menus otherwise written entirely in Spanish. The reason for this is that years back many Mayan people fled to English-speaking Belize to escape persecution in their homeland. While there, they assimilated many of the foods from Belize into their repertoire of cooking. This style of cooking the beans and rice together remained popular as an inexpensive main course upon their return to their native soil. As a side dish, this is perfect to go along with spicy Latin American–style grilled entrees. Grilled Plantain Tostones (see page 101) make a perfect garnish for Rice and Beans.

SERVES 6 AS A SIDE DISH

⅔ cup dry red or black beans (2 well-drained cans of cooked beans may be substituted)

3 cups water (to cook the beans)

1½ tablespoons vegetable oil

2 tablespoons chopped white onion

¼ cup chopped sweet red pepper

1 teaspoon minced jalapeno or serrano chile

2 cloves garlic, peeled and smashed

1¼ cups long-grain rice (not converted)

1 teaspoon chopped fresh thyme or ½ teaspoon dried thyme

1 teaspoon salt

½ teaspoon black pepper

1 13-ounce can unsweetened coconut milk (1½ cups)

⅓ cup water

Chopped cilantro for garnish (optional)

1. Cook the dry beans in 3 cups water until completely cooked through. Drain.

2. In a preheated heavy saucepan, Dutch oven or deep skillet, add the oil and then fry the onion, peppers, chile, and garlic for 1 minute, stirring well. Add the rice and continue to cook for 2 minutes, stirring constantly. When the rice has begun to turn opaque with a little browning, add the thyme, salt, pepper, coconut milk, and water.

3. Bring to a boil and add the beans, stirring to mix.

4. Cover tightly, reduce the heat to simmer and cook 15 minutes more. Remove from the heat, leave the lid on and steam for 15 minutes more.

5. Stir to mix and serve. Garnish with cilantro.

GRILLED PLANTAIN TostonEs

PLANTAINS ARE A POTATO-LIKE member of the banana family consumed throughout the New World. Tostones are twice-cooked discs or patties of plantain that are usually first boiled and then fried. This grilled version will garner a lot of comments, is lighter and makes a good starch or garnish to accompany char grilled, spicy foods. See photo on page 37.

ENOUGH FOR 4 TO 6 SERVINGS

1 clove garlic, smashed, peeled and minced

2 tablespoons vegetable oil

2 large plantains, ripened yellow but not too soft

2 quarts water with 1 tablespoon salt

1 tablespoon of your favorite dry rub (see pages 14–20) or salt and pepper to taste

1. Combine the garlic and oil to infuse the flavor.

2. Make an incision through the skin of the plantain and along the length. Remove the peel and cut into 1½-inch sections.

3. Cook the pieces in the boiling salted water until fork tender but not mushy. Drain and cool.

4. Place a piece of the cooked plantain cut-side down on a cutting board or countertop. Carefully smash with the back of a pan or with the heel of your hand, to form a round disc about ½ inch thick. Continue with the rest.

5. Brush with the garlic oil and season with the dry rub or salt and pepper.

6. Cook over coals or flame on moderate heat until the first side has browned with nice grill marks. Turn over and cook the second side.

7. Serve garnished with chopped cilantro or green onions or use the tostones to garnish other dishes.

Yam or Sweet Potato TumbleWeed

I FIRST DEVELOPED THIS RECIPE to go with Red Chile–Apple Cider Glazed Pork Chops (see page 39) and it also works well with many other smoked or grilled recipes. Yams and sweet potatoes are both New World ingredients that are used in Latin American cooking. The sweet aromatic spices and the hint of chile make a perfect complement to spicy and smoky flavors.

SERVES 6

2 pounds yams or sweet potatoes

4 tablespoons melted butter

½ recipe Sweet Spice Fruit Rub (see page 20) with double the ancho chile powder and salt

1. Preheat oven to 400 degrees.

2. Peel the yams and cut (by hand or using a mandoline) into large shoestring julienne (if they are cut too fine the yams will get mushy when cooked).

3. In a bowl, toss the cut yams with the melted butter, then mix in the dry rub seasoning. Toss well to evenly coat.

4. Place in a large casserole or roasting pan and cover tightly with foil.

5. Bake at 400 degrees for 20 minutes. Carefully remove the foil (watch out for the very hot steam), stir and bake for 15 to 20 minutes more, stirring once or twice, until the yams are cooked through and a little browned around the edges. Serve immediately.

NOTE: You may do the first step of cooking with the foil cover in advance and then do the final uncovered cooking just before serving to help with timing.

FIRE-ROASTED Corn

IN MEXICO, THIS DISH IS SOLD on the street and called *elotes*. There, it is usually spread with mayonnaise or sour cream, spiked with lime juice and chile powder, and then finished with a crumbly cheese such as Cotija or queso fresco. Simply dressed with only butter, salt and pepper; a flavored butter like Chipotle Herb Butter (see page 84); or Mexican style, Fire-Roasted Corn is a great complement to any grilled meat. The corn is sweeter than boiled corn and the subtle smokiness gives an exotic edge to this basic food.

5 to 6 ears of corn (or 1 ear per person)

1. Cut the silk that is on the outside of the husk if you like. Please DO NOT open the cornhusk, soak it, or remove the inner silk. These steps are unnecessary and may cause the corn to taste musty.

2. Preheat a wood, charcoal, or gas grill; oven broiler (high); or oven (450 degrees).

3. Begin cooking the ears. For the grill or broiler, rotate often and cook until the outer husks are well charred and the corn kernels give a little when squeezed, about 7 to 10 minutes. For the oven, place on the center rack and bake, rotating 3 or 4 times, until the outer husks are slightly brown and crispy and the corn kernels give a little when squeezed, about 15 to 18 minutes. (The more ears in the oven at one time, the longer it will take.)

4. Allow the corn to steam in its husk for about 5 or 6 minutes and then remove the husk. The silk will remove easily while husking after the corn is roasted.

FIRE-ROASTED CORN FLaN

A SIMPLE YET SATISFYING COMFORT FOOD; I adapted my Grandma Hoyer's recipe for scalloped corn by fire roasting the ears and adding chiles, herbs and cheese. Flan is an egg custard that is usually sweetened and served as a dessert popular throughout Latin America; however, this reinterpretation as a savory side dish may start a new tradition. This recipe may also be prepared wrapped in cornhusks like tamales* and grilled for a contemporary Southwestern twist.

SERVES 6 TO 8

$4\frac{1}{2}$ cups fire-roasted fresh corn kernels, 5 to 6 ears (see page 103)

$1\frac{1}{2}$ cups heavy cream, divided

$1\frac{1}{2}$ teaspoons arrowroot powder or cornstarch

1 to 2 tablespoons chipotle chiles in adobo, minced OR $\frac{1}{3}$ cup chopped, roasted New Mexican green or poblano chiles

6 tablespoons unsalted butter

$\frac{1}{2}$ cup bread crumbs or finely crushed corn tortilla chips (omit the butter in step 3 if using chips)

$\frac{1}{2}$ cup thinly sliced green onions

1 clove garlic, peeled and minced

1 tablespoon chopped fresh marjoram or sage

4 large eggs, well beaten

1 cup grated Monterey Jack, Mexican queso asadero, cheddar or fontina cheese, (or replace $\frac{1}{3}$ of the above cheeses with Cotija, romano, Parmesan or Asiago for a sharper flavor)

1 teaspoon salt

Black pepper to taste

1. Preheat oven to 350 degrees.

2. Puree half the corn with $\frac{1}{2}$ cup cream, arrowroot powder and chipotle in a food processor.

3. Melt the butter and combine $\frac{1}{3}$ of it with the bread crumbs. In the pan with the remaining butter, add the green onions and sauté for 2 minutes, add garlic and herbs and cook for 2 minutes more.

4. Place all of the corn, onions and garlic in a bowl and mix well. Stir in eggs, remaining cream and cheese. Season with salt and pepper.

5. Pour into a lightly buttered 9 x 13-inch baking dish, or 8 individual ovenproof ramekins or soufflé cups. Sprinkle with bread crumbs and bake 40 to 50 minutes for the pan, 25 to 35 minutes for ramekins until the topping is golden brown and the flan is set but not overly firm (it should wiggle a little when shaken).

NOTE: *If fresh corn is not in season, you may use good-quality frozen kernels. Rinse the corn kernels under cold water until thawed, then place on a lightly-oiled baking sheet in a 425-degree oven for 8 to 10 minutes, or until they show a slight golden-brown color around the edges.*

*TO MAKE GRILLED TAMALES, soak 12 to 18 cornhusks in warm water until soft and pliable. Place about 3 tablespoons of uncooked flan mixture (omit the bread crumbs) in the center of each husk. Carefully fold to seal in the flan and secure with a strip of cornhusk or twine. Place on grill over low or indirect heat, loosely cover with foil or an ovenproof lid or pan to trap the heat and moisture, and cook for about 25 to 35 minutes, turning several times during cooking. See photo page 25.

Fire-Roasted Corn Flan

COCONUT CURRIED RICE
& BLACK-EYED PEAS

THIS IS MY VERSION OF "RICE AND PEAS" that is served throughout the Caribbean. It makes a perfect side dish to accompany Jerked Pork (see page 60), Jerk-Seasoned Grilled Chicken Quarters (see page 44) or any grilled or smoked main dish. The original island recipe uses green pigeon peas, which are available in some areas, and you could also substitute black, red or white beans in place of the black-eyed peas called for. I often prepare this dish in advance, chill it and then toss it with Citrus-Ginger Dressing (see next page) and serve it as a salad.

SERVES 6 TO 8

2 tablespoons vegetable or olive oil

1⅓ cups long-grain white or basmati rice (not converted rice)

1 sweet bell pepper (red, green, yellow, etc.), diced in small, bite-sized pieces

½ inch peeled ginger, sliced in 3 slices

1 clove garlic, minced

1 whole Scotch bonnet or habanero chile OR 1 teaspoon bottled Caribbean chile sauce (optional—use the chile whole and it will flavor without adding too much heat)

1 teaspoon fresh or ½ teaspoon dried thyme

2 to 3 teaspoons yellow curry powder, mild or spicy

Generous pinch of ground cloves

4 green onions (scallions), thinly sliced

2 teaspoons Worcestershire sauce

1 teaspoon ketchup

1 13-ounce can unsweetened coconut milk

1 cup chicken broth or water

½ cup diced ripe tomato (canned diced tomatoes work well)

1½ cups cooked black-eyed peas, pigeon peas or black beans (if using canned peas or beans, drain and rinse)

1½ teaspoons salt

¼ cup chopped cilantro or parsley (omit if making the salad version)

1. Heat the oil over medium-high heat in a saucepan, deep skillet, or small Dutch oven. Add the rice and fry, stirring constantly until the rice begins to turn opaque-white and a touch of brown color develops.

2. Add the sweet pepper and ginger and continue frying for another minute. Add garlic, chile, thyme, curry powder, ground cloves and green onions. Cook 30 seconds more, stirring well to prevent burning.

3. Temporarily remove from the heat and carefully stir in the Worcestershire sauce, ketchup, coconut milk, broth or water, tomato, black-eyed peas and salt. (Beware, the rice is very hot and the liquids will splatter and steam.) Stir well to mix.

4. Return to the heat and bring to a boil. Stir once, cover tightly and reduce the heat to simmer. Cook for 15 minutes, remove from the heat and allow to steam (keep covered, no peeking) for 10 to 12 minutes more.

5. Remove the cover, add the cilantro, and gently fluff the rice with a fork or large spoon held perpendicular to the pan. Remove the ginger slices and the chile, if using. Serve immediately or spread out in a larger pan and chill quickly in the refrigerator to use for making a salad.

CITRUS-GINGER DRESSING

1 teaspoon fresh peeled ginger, crushed and finely minced

½ teaspoon finely minced garlic

2 tablespoons orange juice

1 tablespoon lime juice

2 teaspoons rice or apple cider vinegar

2 tablespoons cilantro or flat-leaf parsley

½ teaspoon salt

Dash of Worcestershire sauce

Generous dash of bottled Scotch bonnet, habanero or other hot sauce (optional)

¼ cup vegetable oil

1. Combine all ingredients and stir or shake to blend. Store in the refrigerator up to several days.

POTATOES & ChiLeS
BAKED WITH GARLIC & SOUR CREAM

THIS IS A RECIPE THAT I CREATED when visiting my friends, Robert and Cynthia, in San Miguel de Allende, Mexico. I used ingredients that I purchased in the market to complement a spicy Mexican menu. The potatoes and sour cream contrast nicely with fiery dishes and the mild chiles tie it all together. This casserole may be prepared in advance and reheated to go with most grilled main courses.

SERVES 6 TO 8

1 3/4 pounds waxy potatoes, peeled and sliced in 1/4-inch-thick rounds (I prefer white, red rose or Yukon gold varieties)

2 quarts water

1 tablespoon + 2 teaspoons salt

Butter or vegetable oil to grease the pan

2 cups (16 ounces) sour cream

1 cup heavy or whipping cream

1/2 teaspoon freshly ground black pepper

8 cloves garlic, peeled and cut in half lengthwise

2 poblano chiles, roasted, peeled, seeded and cut into 1/4-inch-thick, long strips (you may substitute Anaheim or New Mexico green chiles)

1. Par-cook the potatoes by boiling in the water with 1 tablespoon salt until almost cooked through but still very firm and a little crunchy in the center of the slices (about 6 to 8 minutes). Drain immediately.

2. Grease a casserole or baking dish with the butter or oil.

3. Combine the sour cream, cream, 2 teaspoons salt and pepper and mix until smooth.

4. Layer a small amount of the cream mixture to cover the bottom of the casserole. Arrange the potato slices in the casserole, interspersing the garlic so that it is evenly distributed. Scatter the chile strips over the potatoes and cover with the remaining sour cream mixture.

5. Bake at 350 degrees for 25 to 35 minutes until the cream has thickened with a little browning on the top and the potatoes are tender.

6. May be served immediately or cooled for later reheating.

Potatoes and Chiles Baked
with Garlic and Sour Cream

Desserts

WHAT OUTDOOR COOKOUT is complete without a great dessert? Many times, I will plan the dessert first and then create a menu to complement it. Regardless of your menu planning approach, you will want a dessert that is fairly simple to prepare and coordinates well with the other dishes being served. The following recipes were chosen to compliment grilled menus. They include some fruit desserts, chocolate, ice cream and even several that are prepared by using the grill. Enjoy!

Grilled Fresh Pineapple

GRILLING A PINEAPPLE may seem like an unusual treatment for this tropical fruit; however, the sweet, caramelized flavor from the intense heat blends well with the natural tartness of the fruit and the subtle smokiness from the fire. Add the aromatic spices from the dry rub and you have a delicious stand-alone dessert or a perfect topping for ice cream like Avocado-Lime (see page 117), vanilla, cinnamon or coconut. This method even sweetens up a pineapple that is not quite ripe. You can also use unsweetened, canned pineapple slices if there are no fresh ones available. Try it in your favorite pineapple upside down cake recipe too.

1 medium-sized, ripe pineapple

1 tablespoon vegetable oil or cooking spray

2 to 3 tablespoons Sweet Spice Fruit Rub (see page 20)

1. Cut the top and skin off the pineapple with a sharp knife.

2. Slice in half lengthwise, remove the core and slice ¼- to ⅜-inch-thick slices.

3. Brush the slices to lightly coat with the oil or spray with the cooking spray.

4. Sprinkle each slice with some of the dry rub.

5. Grill over medium heat until nice marks develop and the sugar in the dry rub begins to caramelize. Turn over and cook the opposite side the same.

6. Serve warm or cool. This can also be saved for later.

Grilled Fresh Pineapple with Ice Cream

Coconut Cornbread Shortcake
with Fresh Berries

THIS FAMILIAR DESSERT is a favorite at any outdoor cookout or picnic. My version includes some of the favorite flavors of tropical Latin America and the Caribbean—coconut, cornbread and berries with citrus. You could also substitute other tropical fruits or Grilled Fresh Pineapple (see page 110). The shortcake may be baked in one pan and cut for serving, or it could be divided into small tart pans or large muffin tins for baking individual cakes.

MAKES 8 SERVINGS

1¼ cups yellow cornmeal

1 cup all-purpose flour

1½ teaspoons baking powder

¼ teaspoon baking soda

½ teaspoon salt

⅓ cup sugar

1 stick (½ cup) unsalted butter

½ cup sour cream or plain yogurt

1 cup unsweetened coconut milk or whole milk

3 eggs, well beaten

2 teaspoons Mexican or other premium vanilla extract

⅔ cup shredded coconut, lightly toasted

2 cups fresh berries

1 cup whipped cream

1. Combine the first 6 ingredients, and mix well.

2. Cut the butter into small pieces and then cut into the dry mix with a pastry blender, fork or by pulsing in a food processor, until the consistency of coarse cornmeal.

3. Mix the sour cream with the milk until smooth, mix in the eggs and vanilla and combine well.

4. Slowly pour the liquid into the dry mix and gently stir or fold to combine (do not over mix, it will make the shortcake tough and chewy, you only need to moisten and combine everything).

5. Fold in the coconut and place in a baking pan or individual tart shells or large muffin cups; 1½ inches deep for pans and 2 inches for muffin cups.

6. Place in a preheated 400-degree oven and bake for 20 to 25 minutes, or until a toothpick inserted in the center comes out clean.

7. Finish the shortcake with fresh berries and whipped cream for serving.

NOTE: You may split the shortcake, cream and berries into two layers, as shown in the photo, for serving if you prefer.

*Coconut Cornbread Shortcake
with Fresh Berries*

CARAMEL APPLE TART
WITH FIRE-ROASTED GREEN CHILES

CHILES AND APPLES FOR DESSERT? It is not as strange as it may seem. I first created this recipe in a farmers market cooking class in Santa Fe. We were planning an apple dessert and had some beautiful green chiles left. Not wanting to waste the chiles, we decided to use them with the apples and the results were astonishing! I have had a number of requests for the recipe. The sweet richness of the caramel and the tartness of the apples effectively temper the chile heat, although it is still evident if you start with hot chiles, which I recommend.

MAKES 2 8-INCH TARTS OR 1 9-INCH DEEP-DISH, TWO-CRUST PIE

2 Tart Shells (see page 116)

2 cans sweetened condensed milk

1 tablespoon Mexican or other premium vanilla extract

¼ teaspoon salt

2 tablespoons granulated sugar

½ teaspoon ground cinnamon

Pinch of ground cloves or anise seed

4 or 5 tart apples (Granny Smith, Rome, pippin, Braeburn, Gala, etc.), peeled, cored and thinly sliced

1 teaspoon lemon or lime juice

3 or 4 hot New Mexico green chiles, fire-roasted, peeled, stemmed, seeded and chopped (for a milder version, substitute Anaheim chiles or 2 to 3 poblano chiles)

½ cup lightly toasted pine nuts or almond slivers (optional)

1. Pre-bake the tart shells at 400 degrees for 6 minutes, set aside (for the deep-dish two-crust version, only pre-bake the bottom shell).

2. In a heavy saucepan, heat the condensed milk to boiling; reduce the heat to a very low boil and cook, stirring occasionally, until a light golden brown color has developed. Remove from the heat and stir in the vanilla.

3. Mix the salt, sugar and spices together.

4. Sprinkle the apple slices with the lemon juice and then toss with the sugar mix.

5. Arrange the apple slices in layers with the chiles, pour the caramel over the apples and top with the nuts (if using).

6. Bake at 350 degrees for 25 to 30 minutes until the filling is bubbling and has deepened in color.

7. Let sit for 15 to 20 minutes or longer before cutting and serving.

Caramel Apple Tart with
Fire-Roasted Green Chiles

Tart Shells

THIS CRUST RECIPE, used for the Caramel Apple Tart on page 114, is a practically fool-proof method, so that the piecrust-challenged, like me, can produce a good tasting crust. It uses cream cheese for moisture and the egg yolks and butter provide plenty of rich flavor. You will find the resulting dough is very forgiving and does not require the exacting attention to detail that the traditional shortening and ice water method require. While not quite as flaky as the other method, the texture is still quite elegant and I prefer the flavor. Keeping the ingredients as cool as possible, minimal working of the dough once the flour is incorporated and adhering to the resting step will give you excellent results every time and this dough does not require exceptional skills with the rolling pin. You may press the crust into the pie pan with your fingers to insure a good fit. Try using this crust for any of your favorite pie and tart recipes.

MAKES 2 8-INCH SHELLS OR 1 9-INCH DEEP-DISH

2 ¼ cups all-purpose flour

2 tablespoons granulated sugar

½ teaspoon salt

1 ½ sticks (¾ cup) unsalted butter

4 ounces cream cheese

2 egg yolks, well beaten

1. Sift the flour, sugar and salt together and set aside.

2. Cream the butter and cream cheese until fluffy. Slowly add the eggs yolks and whip for 1 minute to more fully incorporate.

3. By hand, gradually mix in the flour mixture a little at a time until moistened.

4. Divide in two equal parts, flatten into circular discs about ½ inch thick, wrap tightly and refrigerate for 30 minutes to 1 hour.

5. Place each disk between two pieces of wax paper or baker's parchment and flatten with a rolling pin to ¼ inch thick.

6. Carefully fold in half, place in a tart or pie pan and unfold. Press the crust into the pan and around the edges, then trim the edges.

Avocado-Lime Ice cream

WHILE NOT TYPICAL of the thirty-one flavors, avocado works surprisingly well as an ice cream flavor. The light green color is appealing and the creamy richness of the fruit adds a smooth texture. The touch of lime brings out a brightness resulting in a refreshing and satisfying dessert to round out any picnic or fiesta menu. Be sure to use ripe avocados. Avocados will ripen more quickly when stored in a paper bag and should be soft and creamy to the touch.

MAKES A LITTLE OVER ½ GALLON

4 large, ripe avocados

1 quart whole milk

1½ teaspoons arrowroot powder or cornstarch

1 quart half-and-half

½ teaspoon salt

1 cup sugar

1 whole egg + 2 egg yolks, well beaten

2 teaspoons lime zest, finely minced

3 tablespoons lime juice

1. Peel and pit the avocados. Pass them through a food mill or a potato ricer or puree in a blender with a little of the milk to make a smooth consistency.

2. Blend the arrowroot powder with ¼ cup of the cold milk until smooth.

3. Combine with the milk, half-and-half, salt and sugar.

4. Warm over medium heat while stirring well, until almost boiling.

5. Carefully combine 1 cup of the hot mixture with the eggs to temper.

6. Mix the tempered eggs and the rest of the milk together, and bring to a gentle boil. Stir in the avocado puree, reduce heat and simmer for 5 minutes more while stirring constantly. Remove from the heat and mix in the lime zest and juice.

7. Cool completely and place in an ice cream maker; freeze according to manufacturer's instructions.

GRILLED BREAD PuDdInG

THIS VERSION OF BREAD PUDDING actually grills the bread slices, and is an inexpensive and simple way to create a rich dessert. Bread pudding keeps well and it may be reheated in the oven or microwave.

SERVES 6 TO 8

½ cup dried fruit (raisins, currants, cherries, apricots, cranberries, apples, etc.)

About ¼ to ⅓ cup sweet wine (sherry, Madeira, port, Marsala, etc.), or apple juice

1¼ pounds small-diameter, crusty bread, sliced ⅜ to ½ inch thick (you may use a larger diameter loaf, just cut the slices in smaller pieces)

3 tablespoons melted butter

1 cup granulated white or raw sugar

2 cups water

1½ cups heavy cream

Dash of salt

1 teaspoon ground cinnamon

½ teaspoon ground allspice

¼ teaspoon ground cloves

1 tablespoon Mexican or other premium vanilla extract

2 tablespoons butter

½ cup pecans, almonds, walnuts, or pine nuts, lightly toasted and coarsely chopped

NOTE: Cut the larger fruits in small pieces.

1. Soak the dried fruit in enough sweet wine or apple juice to cover the fruit.

2. Brush the bread slices with butter to lightly coat.

3. Toast the bread on a medium-hot grill until golden brown. (You may also do this in a 400-degree oven.)

4. Place sugar in a heavy saucepan preheated to medium-low and allow it to melt. Stir by tilting the pan or by using the back of a spoon to avoid introducing air to the sugar, which will cause cooling and crystallization.

5. Continue melting sugar until it is caramelized to a deep, golden brown and smooth with no crystals (beware, the hot melted sugar can cause severe burns).

6. Remove from the heat and carefully add the water. Return to the heat and boil, stirring until sugar dissolves.

7. Add cream and salt and reduce to a low boil. Cook for 12 to 15 minutes, or until mixture just begins to thicken. Add cinnamon, allspice, cloves, vanilla and 2 tablespoons butter. Stir well and remove from heat.

8. In a buttered or oiled rectangular baking pan, place a layer of some of the bread slices, some of the soaked dry fruit and chopped nuts. Repeat layers until all of the bread, fruit and nuts have been used. Pour any remaining soaking liquid over the bread.

9. Pour the caramel mixture over the top using a ladle and making sure all of the bread slices are well coated.

10. Bake at 375 degrees for about 30 to 35 minutes, until the top of the pudding is golden brown. (The center should still be moist and gooey.)

11. Serve warm, garnished with whipped cream, ice cream, or drizzled with powdered sugar frosting.

Grilled Bread Pudding

MEXICAN CHILE-ChocolAtE cAkE

THE AZTEC NOBILITY first enjoyed the magical combination of chiles and chocolate, although they usually consumed it without any sweetening before the Spanish started cultivating sugarcane in the New World. This is an easy yet delicious cake that uses only a small amount of flour. Ground almonds are part of its structure as well as a flavor addition. If you are timid about the chile, by all means, leave it out; however, you will be missing an exciting component of the taste. The mild ancho chiles are more about flavor than heat.

6 TO 8 SERVINGS

10 ounces Mexican chocolate (Mayordomo is my favorite brand) or semisweet chocolate + 1 teaspoon cinnamon

2 tablespoons strong hot coffee

1 stick (½ cup) unsalted butter, at room temperature

½ cup sugar

3 egg yolks

3 egg whites

Pinch of salt

2 tablespoons sugar

½ teaspoon almond extract

1 teaspoon Mexican vanilla or other premium vanilla extract

1 to 2 tablespoons ancho chile powder, lightly toasted (for a hotter chile hit, use guajillo or New Mexican red)

⅓ cup toasted almonds, finely ground

½ cup all-purpose flour, sifted

1. Preheat oven to 350 degrees.

2. Melt chocolate in coffee.

3. Cream the butter with a mixer until fluffy, add ½ cup sugar and continue beating for 1 minute. Beat in egg yolks one at a time until well incorporated.

4. Beat egg whites on high with salt until soft peaks form, gradually add 2 tablespoons sugar and beat until stiff peaks are formed and the whites are shiny.

5. Blend the warm melted chocolate mixture, extracts, chile powder and almonds into egg yolk mixture and then fold into egg whites alternating with the flour. Continue gently folding until all is incorporated.

6. Place in well-buttered and floured 8-inch cake pan and bake for 35 minutes or in individual soufflé cups and bake for 25 minutes. Cake will still move slightly in center when done. Garnish with powdered sugar and cinnamon or more chile powder or whipped cream along with toasted almonds or shaved chocolate.

Mexican Chile-Chocolate Cake

Mocha Flan

FLAN IS A DESSERT that originated in North Africa and the Spaniards brought it to the New World. Flan is an egg custard that is baked in a water bath with caramelized sugar and can be flavored with many ingredients. This recipe uses chocolate, another New World ingredient, and coffee, grown in many Central and South American countries. The comforting simplicity of this dessert makes it perfect to end a rich and spicy meal from the grill.

MAKES 8 SERVINGS

¾ cup sugar for caramel sauce

2 whole eggs + 6 egg yolks

2 teaspoons Mexican or other premium vanilla extract

3 cups whole milk

¾ cup cream

1½ tablespoons instant espresso powder dissolved in ⅓ cup very hot water OR ⅓ cup strong brewed espresso

½ cup sugar

Dash of salt

6 ounces Mexican chocolate (you may substitute semi- or bittersweet chocolate), chopped coarsely

1. Place the sugar for the caramel sauce in a heavy skillet. Heat over medium-high heat and melt the sugar, stirring frequently with back of a large spoon, pressing the unmelted sugar into the caramel. Keep cooking the sugar until it is a uniform, clear and deep golden color. Immediately ladle the caramel into individual custard cups, ramekins or a 9-inch pie pan to cover the bottom, being extremely careful not to splash any of the caramel on you. Cool.

2. Preheat oven to 325 degrees.

3. Whisk the eggs, yolks, and vanilla in a bowl.

4. Mix the milk, cream, coffee, sugar, salt and chocolate in a saucepan and heat gently, stirring frequently, until the chocolate is melted and the liquid is about to boil. Remove from heat.

5. While whisking the eggs, slowly add 1 cup of the hot milk mixture and mix well to temper the eggs. Pour mixture into remaining hot milk while stirring well.

6. Pour the liquid into the custard cups, ramekins or pie pan. Place in a large roasting pan and fill halfway up the side of the containers with very hot water. Bake for about 50 minutes or until the custard still wiggles, but is set. Remove from the pan, cool at room temperature and then refrigerate.

7. To serve, slide a sharp knife around the outer edge of each flan when at room temperature (about 20 to 30 minutes) and then invert on a serving plate.

MEnU sUggESTIOns

THE RECIPES IN THIS BOOK may be combined any way you wish. You may even want to include some of your favorite recipes from another source too. There is no right or wrong combination, so please suit your own tastes. The following are some suggestions of recipe combinations from the book that, in my opinion, work well together. There are many more possible combinations.

Menu #1
Lamb Chops Adovada
Fire-Roasted Corn Flan (Tamale Variation)
Avocado Grapefruit Salad
Grilled Bread Pudding

Menu #2
Jerked Pork, Island Style, or Easy Jerk-Seasoned Chicken
    Quarters
Grilled Plantain Tostones
Tropical Fruit Salsa
Coconut Curried Rice and Black-Eyed Peas
Coconut Cornbread Shortcake with Fresh Berries

Menu #3
Ultimate Char Grilled Steak with Mushrooms, Roasted Chiles
    and Caramelized Onions or Gaucho Beefsteak with
    Chimichurri
Red Chile Caesar Salad with Grilled Garlic Croutons
Fire-Roasted Corn Topped with Smoky Chipotle Herb Butter
Potatoes and Chiles Baked with Garlic and Sour Cream
Avocado Ice Cream

Menu #4
Smoked Whole Chicken with Garlic, Herb and Cumin Marinade
Gazpacho Vegetable Salsa (enough to serve as a side dish)
Grilled Yellow Potato and Roasted Pepper Salad
Caramel Apple Tart with Fire-Roasted Green Chiles

Menu #5
Grilled Crab Rellenos with Fire-Roasted Tomato Sauce
Black Bean and Fire-Roasted Chile Salsa
Jicama Fiesta Slaw
Grilled Calabacitas
Grilled Pineapple with Vanilla Ice Cream

Menu # 6
Orange-Flavored Smoked Turkey Legs
Grilled Pineapple Salsa or Salsa Fresca
Spicy Yam Salad
Rice and Beans
Mocha Flan

Menu # 7
Lime-Marinated Spicy Grilled Salmon
Cilantro-Pumpkinseed Pesto or Charred Cherry Tomato Salsa
Grilled Scallion Garnish
Fire-Roasted Corn Flan
Mexican Chile-Chocolate Cake

RESOURCES

THE FOLLOWING RESOURCES include information for ingredients and equipment.

Food and Cooking Travel Adventures with Daniel Hoyer
www.welleatenpath.com

Santa Fe School of Cooking
116 West San Francisco Street
Santa Fe, NM 87501
cookin@santafeschoolofcooking.com
    or call: 505-983-4511
santafeschoolofcooking.com
Ingredients, equipment and utensils, cooking classes (Daniel teaches here)

Traeger Industries, Inc.
800-872-3437
www.traegerindustries.com
Natural fuel grill/smoker manufacturer and pellet fuel source

Nambe
www.nambe.com
Cast alloy cook and service ware (used in photos on pages 49 and 93)

Above Sea Level
505-473-9766
welovefish@msn.com
The freshest seafood and specialty meats in New Mexico

Blanton's
www.bbqblanton.com
Solid wood supplier for grilling/smoking

WorldPantry.com
866-972-6879
www.worldpantry.com
Dried herbs and spices

Gourmet Sleuth
www.gourmetsleuth.com
408-354-8281
Ingredients and equipment

Bulkfoods.com
www.bulkfoods.com
Bulk herbs and spices

Whole Spice
www.wholespice.com
415-472-1750
Herbs and spices

Spice Barn
866-670-9040
www.spicebarn.com
Dried spices

Frontier Natural Products
www.frontiercoop.com
Spices, seasonings and extracts

Kitchen Market
218 Eighth Avenue
New York, NY 10011
212-243-4433, fax 888-HOT-4433
www.kitchenmarket.com
Spices, herbs and specialty grocery items

Penzey's Ltd.
933 Muskego, WI 53150
800-741-7787; fax 262-785-7678
www.penzeys.com
Spices and herbs

INDEX